THE YOUNGEST OUTLAWS: Runaways In America

In this overall look at the tragic runaway situation—close to one million youths in the United States run away each year—the author interviewed a cross-section of runaways, police, social workers, lawyers, judges, and members of Congress in an attempt to answer the social and legal questions pertaining to runaways. An inside look at two runaway houses and a sobering visit to a home for girls emphasizes the lot of these unhappy, bewildered teenagers. A night patrol through the streets of Manhattan with the unique Runaway Unit of the New York City Police Department illuminates the activities and difficulties all police experience in their encounters with runaways. A comprehensive and enlightening look at the facilities available to runaways— the famous "hotlines," Traveler's Aid—reveals what is—or is not—being done to aid these youths. This book is a significant and important beginning on the road to understanding this escalating problem.

I feel it appropriate to dedicate this book to those who have formed my own "extended family" for so many years: my parents, Lillian and David; my sister, Cheryl (Mrs. Howard Small); my aunt, Juliette Rogolsky; and my maternal grandmother, Anna Rogolsky, a woman of compassion, courage, and faith.

The identities of the runaways have been obscured for their protection. Names from Senate testimony, however, are factual.

THE
YOUNGEST
OUTLAWS

Runaways in America

ARNOLD P. RUBIN

with an Introduction by The Honorable Birch Bayh,
Member, U. S. Senate, Chairman, U. S. Senate Subcommittee to Investigate Juvenile Delinquency.

JULIAN MESSNER
NEW YORK

Published by Julian Messner, a Division of Simon & Schuster, Inc.
1 West 39 Street, New York, N.Y. 10018. All rights reserved.

Library of Congress Cataloging in Publication Data

Rubin, Arnold P.
    The youngest outlaws.
    Bibliography: p. 188
    Includes index.
    SUMMARY: A discussion of runaways in the United States
today including case studies and statistics.
    1. Runaway youth — United States — Juvenile literature.
[1. Runaways] I. Title.
HV741.R83   362.7′4   76-188
ISBN 0-671-32780-1
ISBN 0-671-32781-x lib. bdg.

Printed in the United States of America

CONTENTS

ACKNOWLEDGMENTS

For permission to excerpt and reprint copyrighted material in this book, the author and publisher are grateful to the following:

AP Newsfeatures
    for a newspaper article by AP reporter Dolores Barclay. © 1970 The Associated Press.

E. P. Dutton & Co., Inc.
    for excerpt from "The Life and Death of a Hippie," by Anthony Lukas, published in the book *Smiling Through The Apocalypse*, edited by Harold Hayes. Copyright © 1969 by Esquire, Inc. Reprinted by permission of the publisher, Saturday Review Press/E. P. Dutton & Co., Inc., New York.

Irving Music, Inc.
    for extracts from the lyrics of "Father and Son," by Cat Stevens, published in "Tea For the Tillerman," 1970. © 1970, Freshwater Music Ltd. (England). Controlled in the Western Hemisphere by Irving Music, Inc. (BMI). All rights reserved.

Metro-Help, Inc.
    for "National Runaway Switchboard: The First Six Months," by Metro-Help, Inc., published in *Survey*, 1975.

7

A WORD OF THANKS

There are many people to thank with a book such as this. A complete list of contributors and their contributions would fill many pages.

I want to extend my deep appreciation to all those I had the privilege of interviewing. My thanks especially to those who gave so generously of their time and knowledge. I would particularly like to extend my gratitude to the following people and organizations: John Rector, chief counsel to Senator Birch Bayh's Subcommittee on Juvenile Delinquency; Flora Rothman and Paula Rosenblum, National Council of Jewish Women; Mary Jane Keidel, Teaneck Home; Eleanor Muhlmeyer, New York City Probation Department; Sergeant Greenlay and Police Officers Warren McGinniss and Robert Lopez, the New York City Runaway Unit; Deputy Commissioners Francis Daly and Frank McLoughlin, New York City Police Department; Charles Schinitsky and Ms. Michael Gage, the Legal Aid Society; the Reverend Bruce Ritter, Covenant House; Marjorie Statman, Runaway House; Geoffrey Link, Huckleberry House; Sid Johnson; the Honorable Joseph Williams; Ed Farley, the U.S. Office of Youth Development; Len Tropin, the National Council on Crime and Delinquency; Martin Orlick, Institute for Scientific Analysis; Reverend Fred Eckhardt, Operation Eye-Opener; and Marvin Engel, Traveler's Aid.

While this list is admittedly incomplete, I hope and trust that those additionally kind individuals who have helped will continue their kindness and not think poorly of me for not including them.

However, I would be especially remiss if I did not also add the names of my friends and colleagues at Scholastic Magazines, Inc., who, I think, were as interested in the creation of this book as I. They include Lavinia Dobler, Chief Librarian (now retired), and Elaine Israel, whose own book was this book's godfather.

Finally, I must acknowledge and thank those individuals this book is really about—the teenagers themselves. I'm sorry I couldn't use their real names. Nonetheless, my deepest appreciation and best wishes go to them.

As certainly my thanks go to Iris Rosoff, my editor at Julian Messner, and Lee Hoffman, Executive Editor, for their enthusiasm over this project.

INTRODUCTION

The phenomenon of young people running away from home is a national one, not one confined to a particular area or region of the United States. Every year a million persons under the age of eighteen leave home. According to the latest available estimates, 265,000 youths were arrested in 1973 as runaways. This compares with 199,000 arrests in 1972 and 102,000 arrests in 1966.

Runaways are much younger than many would expect, and they are getting younger each year. In the early sixties, the typical runaway was between 16 and 17. In the past few years, that age has dropped significantly. More runaways are 13 or 14 years old than any other age, and a clear majority are young women. In 1973, 14,000 of those arrested were 12 and under, including nearly 30 per cent, or 4,000, who were 10 and under!

When Mark Twain pictured Huckleberry Finn and Tom Sawyer floating down the Mississippi River, he was responding to a well-established American tradition. Running away has long been a part of America's folklore. For many of our young people, it has served as part of their rite of passage into adulthood.

Today, however, running away is less likely to be a healthy striving for adulthood than an anguished cry for help from a child who may have nowhere to turn. In fact, those who are close to and knowledgeable about today's runaways agree that most are not involved in a healthy search for a mature self-identity. Instead, they are often confused boys and girls who are fleeing serious personal, family, or school problems. These youngsters deserve our help and understanding, but instead they are usually treated with indifference and even hostility. Many of these children are detained in county jails or juvenile hall before returning home.

Although leaving home without parental consent is not a crime, it can have equally serious consequences. Such conduct combined with truancy, curfew violations, and other noncriminal acts known as status offenses can lead to imprisonment in almost every state. In fact, 23 per cent of the boys and 70 per cent of the girls committed to state training schools are status offenders.

Even more serious than the legal consequences of running away are the dangers faced by young runaways on the street. Most runaways flee their suburban family life to go to the city. The children who run look for companionship, friendship, and approval from those they meet. Being young, unfamiliar with the urban scene, and often without money, they are easy marks for gangs, drug pushers, pimps, and other hardened criminals. They are beaten, raped, homosexually assaulted, and become the victims of suicide. Without adequate shelter and food, they are prey to a whole range of medical ills, from respiratory infections to V.D. Testimony developed at our hearings linked the runaway incident to the use of dangerous drugs and to petty theft, especially shoplifting. Runaways often have to sell drugs, their bodies, or steal to support themselves. In this way, the runaway incident often serves as the young person's initial contact with the world of criminal activity. The longer the community ignores the underlying problems which cause it, the greater the likelihood that future behavior will be far more serious.

Tragically, some who run away do so for good reasons. Victims of scandalous parental neglect, including physical and sexual assaults, are filling the ranks of runaways in ever-increasing numbers. Others are also the victims of family disintegration and instability, but of another variety. In some areas 25 per cent of the youth who have left home have been forced to leave. They are the "throwaways." If the economy does not improve, parents unable to cope with their concerns about money and food will undoubtedly aggravate this already pathetic, heartbreaking situation.

Those who run away are confronted with serious problems, but we have not responded to the clear need of providing services for these children. There are very few private agencies that provide help for runaways. Some groups and church organizations do help runaways contact their parents and return home, but they rarely maintain facilities to house a child overnight. Even more rarely do these agencies provide any counseling for the troubled young person.

Although insufficient, there are a few underfunded and understaffed, but highly effective houses in several of our large cities. They provide an alternative to the street for some runaways before they are physically harmed. They provide shelter and immediate assistance, such as medical care and counseling. The counselors in these houses bridge the gap between parent and youth. They encourage youths to contact home and reestablish permanent living arrangements. Though limited by lack of funds and staff, these programs occasionally offer follow-up counseling to help resolve, if possible, the family or personal problems which caused the run initially. Such houses were the models for the Runaway Youth Act, which I introduced in the fall of 1971.

Placed in the communities where runaways tend to congregate, these centers can be an effective means of voluntarily getting young people off the street and back to their homes. They should be equipped to give temporary shelter and intensive short-term counseling, and should be capable of calling on the medical and psychological services of the local community when needed. Most importantly, they should be capable of providing follow-up counseling. While the fragmented statistics now available show that a substantial minority of runaways travel great distances, the majority still tend to run from surrounding suburbs into our major cities. This group of children could be effectively served by a trained staff capable of traveling back to the suburbs to counsel the families of runaways or to suggest more highly specialized psychological or psychiatric help. In short, these programs serve as highly specialized alternatives to the traditional law enforcement methods of dealing with runaways.

This approach obviously does not have universal support. In spite of Senate passage of the Runaway Youth Act in 1972 and 1973, it was not until national attention was focused on the horrifying murders of dozens of runaways in Houston, Texas, that officials in the Executive Branch tempered their opposition to my bill. Fortunately, however, it did become law in late 1974, and today additional centers are providing services, including "hotline" telephone contacts, such as Metroline in Chicago, which handles 2,000 calls a month to young people with problems and their families.

Last year the President opposed full funding of the Act. For 1976, however, I believe that despite such opposition, we will obtain the full $10 million authorized by the Act.

Money alone, we all must recognize, cannot provide the solutions to the problems of young people in trouble. Nor can government provide the affection, responsibility, and other human qualities necessary to make the family relationship work. It can provide, however, an atmosphere supportive of the qualities that cement family life, rather than erode it.

In *The Youngest Outlaws: Runaways in America,* Mr. Rubin provides us with a modern version of the *Adventures of Huckleberry Finn.* This insightful updating is not unnecessarily alarmist. It is, on the contrary, a thoughtful and vivid exposé which underscores the fact that we, as a society, far too seldom respond to the needs of our children in a human and sensible manner.

As we celebrate our 200th birthday, contributions such as *The Youngest Outlaws* will help to assure that our third century will more fully acknowledge that our young people are the nation's most valuable resource.

The Honorable Birch Bayh
Member, U.S. Senate (Dem.-Ind.)
Chairman, U.S. Senate Subcommittee to
Investigate Juvenile Delinquency

I.

One Million a Year

A soft rain swept the streets around the Dupont Circle area in Washington, D.C. It occasionally drove against the windows of the house when the wind came up.

Terry looked beyond the window, sighed, and turned back to the visitor. "Why did I run away?" She repeated the question. It was a question she was used to answering.

"Extreme amount of tension at home, I guess, is the biggest reason. I've thought about running away for two years. I usually don't do things unless I think they're absolutely necessary.

"My older brother—he's twenty-one—had emotional problems: 'tripping' all the time. He was just going crazy; sort of runs in the family. My parents don't let out their anger. Sometimes they should scream at us."

Terry has run away from home before. She is seventeen, and one member of what seems to be a growing legion of young people who run from their homes each year.

No one is exactly sure how many runaways there are in

17

America each year. The figure usually given is between 500,000 and one million. But many feel that that statistic is conservative; some runaways are not reported, and others never come into contact with the police.

In most states, a runaway is generally a person under the age of eighteen who has made a conscious decision to leave home for more than one night without parental permission. Most runaways are between the ages of fourteen and seventeen. The "average" runaway has been described as a fourteen-and-a-half-year-old white female.

Terry blew smoke rings with her cigarette while she spoke. Occasionally she would run her hand down her long, blonde, curly hair. She was dressed in blue jeans, a brown polo shirt, and mud-stained sneakers.

In need of help herself, Terry would like to help others. "Two people can help themselves better than one," she says. "Like counseling other people with the same experiences . . . I could communicate with them."

Weren't her parents worried about her?

Yes, she says, but they haven't tried to get her back. "They let me do pretty much what I want."

"So why run away?" she is asked.

Her green eyes flash.

"The tension," she reminds the visitor. "I definitely won't go back."

No, she says, she hasn't been arrested.

"What about school?"

"I won't go back," Terry says firmly. "I didn't learn anything useful." Instead, she says, she'll take correspondence courses, "where you can pace yourself."

In any event, she will "definitely not go back home."

But Terry is a lucky runaway. She had ended up in a place that is a part of an informal network of scores of "runaway houses" that offer aid and comfort to an estimated maximum of 100,000 young people a year. These houses couldn't handle more people than that, physically or financially.

The particular house Terry is in is located in Washington, D.C. These runaway houses can be found across the United States from New York to California. Without the aid of the house, Terry might have ended up in a reform school. Half the residents of the Indiana School for Girls, for example, have been runaways.

Sometimes running away can be not only dangerous, but fatal.

Houston: August, 1973. A stunned Texas public read the news that soon spread throughout the nation like a forest fire. Over a period of three years, twenty-seven teen-aged boys from the area were enticed to "parties," where they were tortured, sexually abused, and killed.

Many of the victims had been runaways. They were among the nearly 17,000 youths who ran from the Houston area between 1970 and 1972. Police said they could not possibly keep up with such numbers of youth-on-the-run.

Although police say the vast majority of those who run away do eventually return home, such figures may be misleading. Many young people run away again and again.

The runaways have become a national problem. In New York City alone, for example, police have estimated the number of runaways to be as high as 20,000. Although services have been established to aid runaways, many observers believe the problem is a long way from being solved. Runaway shelters are temporary at best, experts acknowledge, unless the root cause of the flight—usually the family situation—is adequately dealt with.

Until this is the case, the experts say, these youths will be back on the streets, or in and out of mental institutions, reform schools, foster homes, detention centers, and runaway houses.

The Houston tragedy may be an extreme case, but the fact remains that running away from home is a risky, sometimes dangerous, business. Those who do not return home, or find safe shelter, or land in the hands of well-meaning friends or relatives, often end up in the grips of pimps, dope pushers, hardened criminals, or street gangs. "Crashing" from "pad to pad," these young people get caught up in a nightmare of loneliness, depression, drugs, panhandling, sex, petty thefts, serious assaults, burglaries, and death.

As a result, runaways become both victims and victimizers. And they see their natural "enemy" as the police. In 1973, for example, over 265,000 teens under the age of eighteen were arrested and charged with being runaways. More than half were girls.

Randy is seventeen. He says he's from Florida and that his father "put me on a bus and told me, 'Don't let me see you again. . . .'" Randy says he has been in and out of boarding schools and institutions since he was eight years old. The reason: "My parents wanted a load off their backs; they thought I had mental . . . problems."

Randy's excursions have taken him, he says, from Florida

to Ohio to Georgia and, finally, when we met him, to the District of Columbia. He says he even tried to stow away to London once, but he got caught.

"I have a problem getting along with people," he admits. "I'm not very outgoing, only talkative." Randy likes to brag about how far he's traveled, and how he "cons" old ladies for money and for aid in stowing away on trains. "I do have to eat, you know," he says.

"It's easy to raise money if you know how to con people; if you work up the correct 'line,'" he says. "For example, I hit them for just a penny first. Then I tell them that ten pennies will get me a hamburger." The result, he says, is before you know it he gets the ten cents, anyway.

Randy, a tall slim youth with dark hair, dark brown eyes, and gold-rimmed "granny" glasses, also acknowledges his home situation—or lack of one.

"My sister and I are adopted. I never knew who my real parents were. I guess you could say my home was 'broke,' but I got used to it."

Randy says he has been "busted" on runaway and juvenile delinquency charges. He also says, perhaps for shock value, that he hasn't "been home longer than three months in eight years." He says he is tired of institutions, however; tired of being tested "like a rabbit."

Although Randy's problem would appear to stem from his home life, not all runaways leave for self-imposed exile because of their parents. Sometimes their problems are imagined or exaggerated. Such was the case of the youngster who left because his parents wouldn't buy him an expensive stereo set.

For many other youngsters, however, the problems are a lot more serious; serious enough to require institutionalization, sometimes unfairly. At one point, for instance, it was said that half of the youth population in mental hospitals was composed of runaways.

Evidence also indicates that the attitudes people hold often work to the runaway's disadvantage. Youngsters on the run will find few offers for help—certainly few without strings attached. The problem over whether or not running away is an illegal act arises because the laws are vague on the subject and differ from state to state. Running away is a status offense. It is not a "crime" as such, because a minor does not commit a crime, per se; he or she commits a delinquent act. A parent can report a child as incorrigible or in need of supervision—these are status offenses. But, in some states, they are actual delinquent acts where the statutes do not make provision for status offenses.

However, while running away is not illegal itself, it can, and often does, lead to other illegal acts, such as being truant. Hence, the difficulty in determining whether running away is against the law.

A recent government study indicated that in twenty-five states and the District of Columbia police can take a child into custody if that child is believed to be a runaway.

The study found itself hard pressed to legally define a runaway. It noted that: "When a state statute attempts to define a 'runaway child,' it is most likely to define such a child in terms so broad as to raise as many—or more—questions as it answers.

"Thus, in Wisconsin, a runaway is '. . . a child who is habitually truant from home. . . .'"

In South Dakota, a runaway is ". . . any child . . . who has run away from home. . . ." In Texas, running away is defined as the "voluntary absence from home without the consent of the parent, guardian or other custodian without the intent to return."

This is why many adults are not eager to share the "crime"; that is, few are willing to be guilty of harboring a runaway, even by offering a night of shelter.

Therefore, the runaway inevitably comes up against the law—and all that the law entails. First, the police. And then a procession of judges, probation officers, social workers, youth workers, psychiatrists, and, possibly, training school personnel. Sometimes, of course, the runaway will be lucky in that he or she may return home before running afoul of the law. Or the errant youngster may run into police, but be returned to home by them.

If parents and child do "make up," all is well. If not, then chances are good the youngster will run away again. And, if this time out, the runaway runs into the arms of a runaway house, chances are equally good he or she may eventually find the way to what may be a better life; perhaps a foster home, for example.

Traditionally the lot of the runaway has been a most difficult one. This fact was reinforced in hearings held in 1972 by a United States Senate subcommittee. The chairman of that subcommittee is Senator Birch Bayh, Indiana Democrat. His group was in large measure responsible for passage of an important piece of legislation dealing with runaways. The legislation is known as the Runaway Youth Act. It became law in 1974. It called for $10 million a year for three years to be spent to help shelter, counsel, and care for runaways.

Before the law was passed, hearings were held. Witnesses —including runaways—told why they thought the new law was needed. They told their stories to Bayh and his Subcommittee on Juvenile Delinquency.

At that time, Bayh noted the seriousness of the problem. "Young people," he said, "receive inadequate or no services when they run away. They often fall into the hands of drug pushers and street gangs, and all too frequently get started down the path to crime.

"If we could discover and treat more of today's runaways," the senator said, "we could (prevent) more of tomorrow's juvenile delinquents."

Bayh's words were echoed by William Treanor, a man associated with Washington's Runaway House. Treanor was a runaway himself when he was young.

"If life on the street is unpleasant," Treanor testified, "the lot of the runaways isn't much better after they are arrested or turned in. Ex-runaways are a major part of the youth population in mental hospitals, reform schools, and detention centers. These young people, often whose only desire is to get away from an intolerable family life, are kept for months . . . even years in these institutions."

The former runaway continued to outline the dimensions of the problem for the senators. "These young people," he said, "pretty much get drawn into the [criminal justice] system because that is all the system offers them. . . . They cannot get any help until they have committed some real or imaginary violation. The critical problem for young people is that if they want to deal with their difficulties, if they want to find a living situation that will help them meet their needs, there is nothing for them." What the government does provide, he said, was jails and institutions.

Therefore, experts say, what should really be a social problem becomes a legal one. Said one Maryland police official, "Our problem is, and I think I can speak from the east coast to [the] west coast and north and south, what are we going to do with runaway juveniles? . . . The officer and patrolman on the beat . . . is sympathetic to this situation. It is the fact that we are the ones that . . . are dealing with them, right off the street. . . . [It] is a family and a social problem, and the police are burdened with it."

One teenager who had run afoul of the police, and who explained her experiences to the senators at the hearings, was a girl named Cathie B. At the time, Cathie was a "client" of a runaway house known as The Bridge. It's located in San Diego, California.

Cathie said she first ran away from home at thirteen, but had run several times since. She said she couldn't get along with her stepfather. He was an "ex-drunk," she said, but he would sneak "drinks" when he was out of the house. When he was not drinking and home, Cathie said, he was "nervous and upset."

The pretty teenager also said her stepfather beat her. "I came home an hour late one day and walked in the house with a friend, and he was going to hit my friend, but my mom got her out of the house before he could. He started

hitting me with a belt buckle and asking me what happened, why was I late?

"At first I lied to him," Cathie went on, "and then he kept
saying I was lying, so I decided to tell him the truth and
he still said I was lying. And at the same time, he is hitting
me.

"Then he said he took it out on my mom, because I
wasn't around, because I was late and he didn't have anybody else to take it out on. He said he didn't care about
me, he cared about my mother.

"I said he didn't care if I was dead, so he went in the
kitchen and got two long butcher knives, and he was going
to stab me. My mom had to wrestle with him for five
minutes. . . . Finally he calmed down and he dropped the
knives. Then he threw shoes at me."

Cathie also said she used to live with her sister and
brother-in-law before her mother married, "because she
[mother] always worked and she didn't want me at the house
by myself all the time."

The first time Cathie ran away, it was to a section in San
Diego, to "this little house. . . . The whole house was just
one room." She ran away with her brother's wife's sister.
"She is fifteen, and we stayed with some guys," Cathie said.
The group included six friends, all eighteen or nineteen
years old.

Cathie said she stayed in this room for two-and-a-half
weeks before she turned herself in to the police.

"See," Cathie explained, "the friends left me. I was like
there by myself, and I didn't know what to do. There was

this one guy that lived in a different house there, and he talked me into going home, so I went home."

Then there was the second time Cathie ran away. This time she stayed with some friends for "about three days." It was in a home. "This guy's parents lived there, too, and he said that they were on vacation. I ran away with another chick, too. He said, 'My mom went on vacation, and the people I was supposed to stay with left, and I can give you a place to stay.' So I stayed there."

The third time Cathie ran away from home was "because me and my stepfather got into an argument because I ate a piece of bacon in my room, and he walked out of the house. . . . We had just got the house, and it was a new rug and stuff.

"So he walked out and me and my mom talked about it, and I asked her, maybe it would be better if I went to live with my sister again . . . until they got things settled. She said, 'No, I wouldn't do that to you.' But a half-hour later, she said, 'Maybe it would be better if you did go and stay with her.' I go, 'How long, a week?' She goes, 'No, about a year.' "

Cathie left her home once again and headed for her sister's house. The initial plan was for her to enroll in a school near her sister. There was one drawback, however. The school cost $1,300. But for Cathie this was good news. She hoped this would cause her parents to want her back home.

"My mom had [written] me a letter that . . . said if she could have, she would have gotten me off the bus . . . and if any chance came up, she wanted to get me home, because she was sorry she sent me away. So I thought if it cost $1,300, that is a bigger chance, she wanted me home. So when I called up, she said maybe my stepfather would call up somebody and get me in school. That really hurt me.

"We tried to talk to somebody and we couldn't. They were going to pay it—$1,300; they must have wanted me gone pretty bad. So I ran away again."

This time Cathie "stayed about five houses down the street with this other chick and two guys. But they lived with their parents, and we would sleep in the car every night . . . when their parents went to work and their little sister and brother went to school, we would sneak in the house and go to sleep."

The fourth time Cathie ran away she was arrested and placed in a juvenile hall. She explained the events that led to her arrest, detention, and eventual referral to The Bridge.

"We went back to my house. You know, I lived in a trailer park. We went back there to see some friends and that was really stupid. We went to this chick's house and this other chick that lived in the trailer park had run away with me, too. So there (were) two of us. The other chick's mother saw her come in the trailer park, so she came up to the house and walked in the door. She knew I had (run) away with her daughter, you know, and she walked in and saw me sitting by the telephone. But her daughter was in the bathroom, and she was asking where Laurie was . . . and I went, 'I don't know, I don't know.' She left, called us a bunch of liars. . . . (Then) she came back. And she tried to get in the bathroom, because that is where we were, and we were hiding from her.

"So," Cathie continued, "Laurie was in the shower, and I pulled the curtains and flushed the toilet and pretended like I was going to the bathroom, and I walked out, so she didn't look in the bathroom.

"We were trying to get away, and her mother was following us everywhere we went, so we had to sneak Laurie over to the gas station. Her mother was following us, so we started hitchhiking, and we were going to come back after her."

It was not too long before the other girl's mother once more caught up with Cathie. And it was not too much longer after that, that Cathie was arrested. Her story continues.

"Me and this guy were hitchhiking, and the mother came back and said she wanted to pick us up. I go, 'No, you will take me home.' She says, 'No, I won't take you home.'

"So we were hitchhiking in front of (this) gas station, and there was a highway patrol in front, and she [the mother] backed up and told them I was a runaway, and the highway patrol came over and picked us up. They called my mother and stepfather, and asked her [Cathie's mother] if they wanted us taken home or to the hall. My stepfather said the hall, and my mom just agreed. So I got taken to the hall and checked over and stuff."

Cathie vividly remembered the day her mother and stepfather committed her to a juvenile hall. She should have. It was her fourteenth birthday.

"It (was) awful," Cathie recalled, "because, like, you run away for help, and you get locked up, you know. They treat you like you are a criminal. They treat you like you did something really wrong. . . . They never counsel you, they don't talk to you, they just—well, you can't talk at all unless you are eating or you are not playing in the gym or something. You can't talk on the way to school, can't talk in the halls, can't talk in the showers or anything."

Further, Cathie said, most of the girls in the hall were there because they had committed crimes more serious than running away. For example, she said, "The chick I was sharing the room with . . . took acid every day, and she got busted with a bunch of it."

Cathie stayed at the juvenile hall two days before her detention hearing. Then, "they said that I could be detained at The Bridge until I went into a foster home—well, for six weeks—and if I don't have a foster home then, then I have to go to the hall again and wait for one. But six weeks came up, and I still hadn't had a foster home, so The Bridge made an exemption for me to stay there until I [could] find a foster home. . . ."

Then Cathie said she tried to reach some sort of understanding with her parents. But that didn't work out, so Cathie had to wait at The Bridge until she could be placed.

"I wanted a family session with my stepfather," Cathie explained, "and my mother. My stepfather wouldn't do it because he said, anything happens, I will just split again, because he thought I was running away because it is fun. So my mother had a family session. We got a little straightened out.

"We were going to try to talk my stepfather into it still. He said no. Like he would get mad at my mother if she talked to me on the telephone or came to see me. He didn't want her to go to the family session. She had to sneak out of the house. And every time he found out about it, he would get really mad at her and yell at her.

"One time," Cathie said, "he got so mad at her for going to see me, and my older brother and sister-in-law came over to the house, and everything just built up between him and me and my sister-in-law, because she would give us some of the attention and he didn't get it at all. He got mad and got in a big hassle with her and hit her, and she has asthma and she had an asthma attack and had to be rushed to the hospital."

That was the story of Cathie B., resident of California, "client" of The Bridge, ninth-grade student. In the course of one year, at the age of thirteen, she ran away from home not fewer than four times.

Along the way she had to live off the proceeds from the sale of stolen goods, or the money ripped off from cigarette machines. Then there was the time she got involved with a group whose religion involved drugs.

"I always used to take speed," she said. "I dropped acid once in awhile, and I smoked dope. I smoked dope all the time." And, she admitted, "I got drunk a lot."

In addition to the personal experiences involved in being a runaway, there is another dimension: the financial side of dealing with runaways.

It cost the San Diego police, for example, $22 to arrest one runaway. By the time expenses were added in for an average eight-day stay for 707 youths detained in a juvenile hall, and a half day of probation officer's time, the total came

31

to a shade under $128,000. (The cost for one youth detained over an average eight-day stay is $181.)

Meanwhile, Cathie B. has become a member of an unenviable "club." This club, which consists of the 500,000 to one million—or more—runaways, also takes in another group.

This group consists of young people who are forced to leave home by their parents. Of the one million runaways in 1974 who were under 18 years of age, some 250,000 were said to have been driven from their homes. There is a name for these young people: the "throwaways."

2.

Throwaways and Runaways

In the 1960s, the youth capital of the United States was reportedly the Haight-Ashbury section of San Francisco, California. This was the time of "flower power," when the Vietnam War protests were reaching their peak.

By the time flower power had wilted in the early 1970s, the youth capital had shifted from west to east. Haight-Ashbury was succeeded by what had once been a haven for Eastern European immigrants decades before: the lower east side of New York City. Only this time, instead of receiving immigrants, the area received youth. And, in addition to receiving "refugees" from the west coast instead of Europe, it also had a different identity. It was no longer the "lower east side." It was called the "East Village."

There were still other changes. In 1968, journalist Anthony Lukas wrote about "The Life and Death of a Hippie." He was known as "Groovy." And, Lukas wrote, "he was an original, a tortured tumbleweed among the flower children, many of whom were products of the manicured lawns and gladiolus beds of New Rochelle and Great Neck (New York). . . .

"Most of the hippies," Lukas wrote, "dropped quite deliberately from suburbia into the East Village and Haight-Ashbury, seeking the bizarre and the immediate. But Groovy was a true dropout from society, who quite by chance found the hippie scene ready to drop into. Two decades ago he would have dropped out anyway and ended at best a gentle, aimless wanderer through America's shantytowns, at worst a leather-jacketed motorcycle tough. In the East Village he was an all-too-easy luminary, reflecting the gleam in the eyes of a thousand runaways. But to have starred in Central Falls (Rhode Island), before an audience of bakers lined up in the windows of a great brick box, among the trucks and filling stations and the railroad tracks and the junkyards—that may have been one of his finest hours."

When Groovy's body was found, it was found with that of the daughter of a prominent family, who also had been beaten to death. The girl, Linda, "quickly became a symbol of the profound alienation of many middle-class youths," Lucas wrote.

But although the middle-class runaways may have received more exposure in the media, the problem cut across other groups in American society.

In fact, you might be able to detect a pattern that began to form. For example, four years after Lukas wrote about Groovy, Sen. Bayh opened his hearings on what had become a national problem. From the outset, one thing became clear. Runaways were no longer running *to* something, such as Haight-Ashbury or the East Village. Instead, they were running *away*. And their numbers were increasing at an alarming rate. Over the four-year period, for example, from about 1967 to 1971, the number of runaways increased 60 per cent, according to figures compiled by the Federal Bureau of Investigation (FBI). "This figure is especially alarming," Bayh noted, "when we realize that the large majority of runaways never have contact with the police, and so are not counted as part of the runaway problem. Thus, police statistics are showing us only the tip of the iceberg."

Of further concern to many people was the indication that the ages of the runaways were getting lower. "In 1963 and 1964," Bayh added, "the most common ages noted for runaways were 16 and 17. In the past few years, that age has dropped to 15. Recently, there has been an alarming increase in the number of very young runaways. In New York City, for example, 43 per cent of the runaways are between the ages of 11 and 14. Indications are that this group may become the single largest runaway age group. Fifty-five per cent of girl runaways in New York City are already in the 11 to 14 age group."

Further insight into the problem was revealed throughout the hearings and in later press accounts. And another group of youths on the run was described: the throwaways. Throwaways are youngsters who are, in effect, kicked out of the house by their parents.

In late 1973, Mary Reinholz, a writer for the *New York News Magazine*, discussed "The Throwaway Children." These were the young people who had gravitated to the East Village after what the author called "the refugees from middle-class affluence [had] flooded the East Village in the '60s. . . ." This new group was different. "Few of the new breed," Ms. Reinholz wrote, "want to be hippies and few think of themselves as runaways. They often call themselves throwaways—throwaways, disposable children tossed out with the trash." These self-styled throwaways, she wrote, began to appear in the East Village about 1970. It was, she noted, "around the time that flower power faded and most of the middle-class kids had headed for The Land or safer cities or home."

But these teenagers were different in other ways as well. "Many," Reinholz wrote, "are unskilled and semi-literate because they grew up in reform and mental institutions or in families and foster homes where they were beaten and neglected. Unlike the privileged kids who preceded them —and who were first initiated into life on the streets by junkies, pimps, and psychopaths—these new young people had lost their innocence long before."

These youths form a sort of army of the unwanted. In fact, one lawyer quoted by Reinholz said, "Nobody wants them. Their parents don't want them, the schools don't want them, and most employers don't want them."

About two years after Bayh's Subcommittee to Investigate Juvenile Delinquency began its hearings into runaways, it issued its final report on the subject. The report did not differ markedly from the testimony presented at hearings two years before. It was, in a sense, a summation of the problem.

"Over a million children leave home without parental consent each year," the report said, "and, living on the streets of strange communities, become easy victims of street gangs, drug pushers, delinquents, and criminals. The tragic murders in Houston of almost thirty young people who disappeared from home has underlined the desperate need for action with regard to the runaway problem. . . ."

The report also dealt with two, by now familiar themes: runaways were getting younger all the time, and they presented a law enforcement problem. The report noted too that the majority of runaways are apparently female, which, as we will later see, presents a different kind of problem.

"As serious as the numbers involved," said the report, "is the developing trend toward younger runaways. Although a few years ago the typical runaway was 16 or 17, today's runaway is probably no more than 15 years old."

The report went on to cite the legal aspects of the runaway problem, especially as it related to juvenile delinquency, law enforcement, and juvenile care.

"Since running away is a juvenile status offense, it has serious legal consequences for the young people involved," the report said. "While the applicable age varies somewhat from state to state, a runaway under 18 years old is subject to arrest, detention in a jail or juvenile hall, and even [placement] in a juvenile institution. Many runaways fall into this pattern: 265,600 were estimated as arrests last year according to the FBI. Running away is the seventh most frequent cause of arrest even though it is only one of the 21 categories of arrest recognized by the FBI which applies only to those under 18."

The report noted where some of the runaways end up. Many, it said, end up in detention facilities (such as juvenile hall or jail). For example, it said that over a period of three years, nearly 5,000 runaways were held an average of eight days each in the juvenile hall in San Diego, California. The report also cited information showing that in 1973 half the inmates in both the Indiana and Illinois Training Schools for Girls were made up of runaways.

"Even more serious," the report went on, "than the legal consequences of running away are the dangers faced by young runaways on the street. Most runaways flee their suburban family life to go to the city. Being young, unfamiliar with the urban scene, and often without money, they are easy marks for the drug pusher, the hustler, or the street thug.

"Testimony developed at the hearings linked the runaway incident to the use of dangerous drugs and to petty theft, especially shoplifting," the report noted. Further, it said, "Runaways often have to sell drugs or steal to support themselves. In this way, the runaway incident often serves as the young person's initial contact with the police and the world of criminal activity."

Then the report issued this warning: "The longer the community ignores the underlying problems which cause it, the greater the likelihood that future behavior will be far more serious."

Whether we call these unfortunate youths runaways or throwaways, one fact remains the same. They are America's children.

Some of them belong to an army of three million young people. This group has been termed "doorstep children" by anthropologist Margaret Mead. In 1973, Dr. Mead described these "doorstep children" in front of a Senate sub-committee on children and youth. This committee was headed by Sen. Walter Mondale, Democrat from Minnesota. The subject of the hearings was: American Families: Trends and Pressures.

Doorstep children, Dr. Mead said, "are teenagers, young people for whom you cannot find any person who can give permission for them to have their tonsils out, who are living without any responsible care by society." And, Dr. Mead added, "Many runaways are a small section of this group."

But these teens have names and faces. And stories to tell in answer to that universal question: Why?

The first time Rick ran away from home he was eleven years old. "That is when I started becoming aware of the problems and the unbearable situation . . . I was around ten, about ten and a half, I guess," Rick once testified.

The story Rick told was of parents who did not live together. He hadn't seen his mother in seven years, the fourteen-year-old boy said. This meant the last time he saw her was when he was about seven. He said he lived with his father and his father's parents. All three, he said, were alcoholics. And when his father was drunk, or even when he wasn't, he would beat him, Rick said. So, eventually, Rick ran away from home. He was eleven.

He went, he said, to "a number of places." The first time he left, he said, "there was like a modernized apartment building with an alleyway in it and a furnace. . . ."

Rick added that there was also "a couch laid out and an unlocked door that didn't have a lock on it where the garbage was kept. I stayed there for one night. The first time I ran away, I . . . wound up right back. They sent my [older] brother after me to drag me back home, because he knew all the places that I went to."

(His brother, Rick added, was also a runaway, and was sent to an institution for using drugs at the age of sixteen.)

Rick described the next time he ran away.

"So I went back to that alley thing again and . . . my dad said [to Rick's brother], 'Listen, go out and get Richard . . . I won't harm him in any way . . . all I want to do is have a chat with him. . . .'"

But things didn't quite work out that way as Rick tells it. "My brother agreed to it and said okay. So my brother came and told me the story about, oh, it is going to be groovy, he doesn't want to hassle you at all. . . . He woke me up in the middle of my sleep, because he knew exactly where the place was. So I walked back with him, and I tried to split from him a couple of times and he caught me. . . ."

Rick sets up the meeting with his father. At the outset, Rick said, his father was calmly brushing his hair. He told Rick, "Just sit down in the living room." His brother reassured him as well. "It is okay, he is not going to harm you," the brother told Rick.

But suddenly the atmosphere changed, as Rick relates it. "So I sat down in the living room and then he [father] comes charging in and just picked me up out of the chair and gave me three or four backhands. . . ."

Rick describes the beatings. His father, he said, "smashed me against the wall, threw me on the floor, started kicking me in the stomach, pulled me up by the hair, threw me in the chair, and just started mutilating my arm. After that, he got started talking to me, because he goes on the basis of hurt now, talk later."

The so-called talk, Rick explains, was decidedly one way. "That was hard, like I didn't even have enough breath to talk, it just came squealing out and stuff.

"Then I just started going back to school after that and I hadn't run away any time. Like that was the last time I had run away when I was eleven years old," Rick said.

Rick ran away from home four times altogether. His ventures lasted from one night to about two and a half weeks. Fortunately, he was able to avoid hunger because he had some money. (Hunger is a constant companion for runaways who have neither money nor contacts.)

In Rick's case, "I didn't get too hungry. I stayed at a friend's house because his room was like in a basement, downstairs, and like the parents' room was upstairs, so they didn't really know."

This didn't completely end Rick's worries, however. "Mainly I was scared of getting caught by the police," he said. "That is what I was always constantly fearing."

Eventually, Rick was made a ward of the court and placed in a runaway house known as Huckleberry House. In the meantime, his father was convicted of assaulting one of Rick's grandparents, and was placed on probation.

In the runaway house, Rick agreed, he was out of a bad home situation. And away from an abusive father.

Becky's is the story of another runaway.

Becky came from a "pretty comfortable" family as she put

41

it. But it was not long before Becky became a client of the Runaway House in Washington, D.C. Her problem, as she described it, was her mother's poor health.

"My mother had been sick since around when I was born," she said. "So it made for a lot of confusion in the family, because she wanted a lot of attention and even tried to battle me for it. They also would have fights and blame it on me."

Becky became a runaway. She was fourteen. And it was not a very pleasant experience.

"I was not really aware of what I was doing," she said. "It was sort of like a friend who was going and agreed to go with me, and I kind of just took off. I did that a couple of times. One time, I did get raped and had some hard times. But I was not really understanding what I was doing and I was not really changing anything."

Then, one Christmastime, when Becky was fifteen, she was arrested. She was put in a youth hall in Florida, where she had gone with a friend. The hall, she said, "was not too comfortable. They did not have any toilets in the rooms, and all they had was little cans; they would not let you out at night, you had to use a can. It was pretty dirty."

Her stay at the hall, however, did come to an end, and she was returned to her home. It was, in a way, adding insult to injury, as she described it.

"I had to pay my plane fare back, and I went to court and got put on probation."

But it was not very long before her home situation turned sour again. Her parents "had had a fight, and then they told me that they thought I was sick and crazy. It really upset me, because they were being really serious about it, and a lot of other things had been building up in me. I thought of leaving."

She did leave.

"I left home, and I was over at a friend's house and we looked at *Quicksilver Times* and found the name of Runaway House and called, and they said come over and talk to them. We had already left home. I went over there and stayed there."

Becky says she then tried to work out the problem with her family through counseling and talking to her parents.

"I started trying to, like, change my problem. I tried to get my parents to agree to family counseling. I called my probation officer regularly and talked to my parents and decided that I wanted to go back home and . . . see if anything could be worked out."

As it turned out, however, things could not be worked out. Becky soon found herself on the road again.

"Eventually, I went back home and they did not agree to family counseling. I stayed home all summer long. Then, in the fall, I just could not really take it much more, because . . . there was just a lot of confusion and fights and things that really upset me. . . .

"So I left again in the fall and went back to Runaway House and tried . . . finding another place to live, like a foster home or tried to get into one of the group foster homes."

But, Becky said, at that point she ran into parental opposition. "My father would not agree to pay for me. Finally, he agreed to give $100 a month to someone who would let me live with them if the court would approve. I did not find anybody like that, that I could do that with."

It was along about this time, as Becky described it, that she became a throwaway child. She got arrested and was returned home, only to leave again—this time at her father's urging, she said.

Her father, she said, "gave me an ultimatum that I could not live at home anymore, and I either had to go to a southern Baptist boarding school or I just could not live at home anymore. So I left again, spent some time living on the street for about a month. . . ."

Eventually, Becky was placed in a foster home. But not before she "got really sick and went through tonsillitis and strep throat . . . and finally ended up on the [hospital] psychiatric ward. . . ."

Becky was not at first aware that her parents had driven her out of the house.

"At first," she said, "I felt like it was an impulse, and I was not aware, you know, of what my problems were. Then, after I had gone to Runaway House and started getting into what I was feeling . . . it was more a feeling that home was really intolerable."

She said she did try to communicate with her parents and did manage to talk to her father "a lot." But she still had difficulty, she said, talking to her mother.

"My mother was really difficult," she said, "because most of the problems were with her. . . . I really felt like she resented my being around."

In fact, Becky said, "Sometimes when I left, she would say, 'Go ahead and go to California and run away,' because she said she had left home when she was 10 years old and I could do it."

As Becky tells it, her mother's words had a profound, and negative, effect on Becky's image of herself.

"Just really," Becky said, "she would make me feel like I was the worse [sic] person in the whole world."

This, in a sense, was the root of Becky's home problem, based on how she said her parents responded to her.

"When I called them up," Becky explained, "I said I was not going to actually leave town. I was going to stay in the Washington area and try to work things out. She suggested that I go away. And there were just a lot of complications around that. So that is where most of my difficulty was, because my father could not really do anything about it, you know. He felt strongly tied to my mother. But most of it was just the way she made me feel, and it was really hard to live with."

Although Becky did eventually get a job working for Runaway House, she was an almost classic example of an average runaway. She was a fourteen year old white female.

Furthermore, she was not running *to* something, but rather away *from* something—in her case, abusive parents. Moreover, she came from what apparently were middle-class origins, although, as William Treanor of Runaway House observed, "there are as many runaways from working class and lower class families as there are from middle class families. . . ."

Those who run *to* something, he added, were "a very, very small minority. It is almost exclusively a problem of run-

45

ning away from the family. . . . I think I have found that it is pretty common for a runaway to come from some kind of fractured family."

Treanor did concede that some kids who run away "do have fantasies that it sounds like such a good idea to hang on the streets of Georgetown (Washington, D.C.), Greenwich Village (New York City), or whatever part of the country they are from." But, again, these people are in the minority.

Treanor's views were reinforced at the hearings by another runaway-youth expert, Brian Slattery of Huckleberry House. "I would say 70-80 per cent have significant family problems. That is what they report when asked, 'why did you leave home?'" Slattery said.

"Those who leave," he continued, "for purposes of traveling and seeing California, and as if the streets of Haight-Ashbury are paved with gold, are probably 5 per cent, if that."

And so the '60s came to an end. There was no gold to be found in the streets of Haight-Ashbury or the East Village. Perhaps there were just some new beginnings, or old endings.

3.

Journeys

Chances are that Mary Vecchio and Karen Baxter probably never knew each other. For one thing, Mary was fourteen when Karen was about ten. For another thing, the two girls were separated by more than time. They were separated by distance as well. Mary was from Florida. Karen was from Massachusetts.

Yet they had three things in common. Both ran away from home. Both were written up in the media. And reportedly both traveled the road of prostitution.

Mary Vecchio and Karen Baxter's paths will never cross. In 1975, Karen Baxter was murdered. Police said she was killed by one of her "customers." Her body was found in a shabby hotel in New York City.

She was fifteen years old.

Meanwhile, Mary Vecchio had spent six months in a juvenile home, after running away from home. She then had some skirmishes with the police, and, at seventeen, was arrested and fined $50 for prostitution.

At the age of nineteen (when this book was being written), Mary reportedly was a switchboard operator in Florida. But her story goes back to the time when she was fourteen and the Vietnam War was still raging. And Karen Baxter was ten years old.

In 1970, then-President Nixon announced a U.S. military "incursion" into Cambodia, in Southeast Asia. The move was an attempt to clean out Communist troops who were using Cambodia as a base against American troops. The move touched off further protests in the United States against the war.

At one such demonstration, at Kent State University in Ohio, four students were shot to death in a confrontation with troops from the National Guard. Kneeling over one of the dead students was a young girl, a look of horror upon her face. Presumably, she was also a college student.

Before long this famous photograph was reproduced in magazines around the country. For millions of Americans, this girl was just another nameless figure in an American tragedy. But for one American man in particular, the girl —pictured on the cover of *Newsweek* magazine—had special significance.

The man's name was Frank Vecchio. He was a carpenter from Florida. The girl on the cover was his daughter, Mary, age fourteen. And she had run away from home.

It was a long way from Kent State in Ohio to a Florida switchboard. And a long time: five years. The years and distance have not made it easier for the carpenter's daughter.

"I've been miserable since Kent State," *Newsweek* quoted

her in 1975. "Not for any political reasons but after all the publicity I've received, I feel the police have been unnecessarily harassing me," she reportedly said.

Mary is alive though, and there is always the chance that she might find happiness some day. But for Karen Baxter, that chance was lost forever one winter night.

"She was a slim, red-haired 15-year-old." With these words, Associated Press reporter Dolores Barclay began the story of Karen's death.

"She smiled invitingly at the cars cruising Third Avenue in the early morning hours. She was a teenage runaway trying to make it as a prostitute. That night one of her customers would choke her to death with a metal chain," the story continued.

The Barclay story was written less than two weeks after Karen's death. It included interviews with the dead girl's mother, her older sister's fiance, and a police officer who had arrested the girl for prostitution.

"She never did anything that bad here," the mother said tearfully at the time. "If they had been more willing to help, my daughter would be alive today," she wept.

"You can't really blame her for wanting to get out of here," said the fiance. He described the area where Karen grew up after her father left ten years before, forcing the family on public aid.

"There is nothing for a growing girl to do around here," said the ex-social worker and friend of Karen. "And she was growing fast. Like the rest of the girls around here, she knew more at nine than a girl somewhere else would know at fifteen."

Karen, said reporter Barclay, was given the choice of living with a relative or being placed in an institution. She headed for New York instead. Her journey, which lasted about a month, ended in death.

The fear of prostitution did not deter Karen, any more than the fear of arrest did. When a policeman told the girl she was under arrest for prostitution, she replied, "Oh. Okay. It's all right. But I'd hate for my mother to find out."

The following morning after her arrest, Karen was back on the street again. She had convinced police she was nineteen and this was her first arrest. That night she was killed.

Karen's tragic fate, unfortunately, has not deterred other young girls from running away. Said one sixteen-year-old when asked if Karen's death had frightened her, "I'm not scared, just hungry."

"A large number," said one policeman, "are victimized by the streets through their own naivete. They more or less permit themselves to be victimized. And this is the principal source of prostitutes in New York City or any other large city."

Those were the words of Officer Warren McGinniss. He is attached to the New York City police runaway unit. He was interviewed by *U.S. News & World Report* magazine a few months after Karen's murder.

McGinniss doesn't believe Karen's death was necessarily in vain. Instead, her example may have had an effect on law enforcement authorities by forcing them to focus more acutely on the dangers faced by juveniles who run away.

A young runaway named "Mouse" testified at the Senate hearings about the same time as Becky did (see Chapter 2). Mouse's case highlights the problems of runaways who can only get help if they commit acts other than running away.

Mouse Norris ran away from home for the first time when he was about fifteen. "I was in the Boy Scouts," he recalled, "and I had just gotten home. I owed my father $20 because he paid for me to go to camp. I had been doing some work, and I did not have the money right offhand and he wanted me to get his money. I did not, so he came at me with an electric cord, and I took off out of the house.

"So," Mouse continued, "I stayed at my godmother's house for a night and a day and then I went home. Things became steadily worse."

It was not long before Mouse became the head of the family in a tragic twist of fate.

"It was, like, my father is a disabled veteran," he said, "and he is receiving a pension. My mother was a registered nurse and she got sick and died in 1968 and the responsibility of the family was left with me."

Mouse was about fifteen at the time.

"My older brother," Mouse explained further, "had left home when he was thirteen. He is now in Lorton Reformatory. I left home. Nothing was ever worked out after I came back home from my godmother's house. So I went on through that year and I just stayed terrified of my father most of the time. So, in May, 1970, I decided I could not take his harassment anymore, because I had been working with the Black Panther Party [a radical political group], and we had differences in that. We could not communicate at all on any level. I decided I just could not take it anymore."

One day, as Mouse told it, he went to school and decided not to return. His plan was to join the Panther party in New Haven, Connecticut. As it turned out, however, they had problems of their own.

"I went down to the bus station, bought a ticket, and went. . . . I stayed at the Panthers . . . But they . . . told me that they could not bother with me as a runaway, because they were already hot and they were being raided pretty regularly. So they put me on the bus and sent me back to Washington."

But Mouse didn't give up. He tried the Panthers in Washington, and "they tried counseling with me, but the counseling was kind of go home, you know, you can help us more if you go home."

Mouse, however, rejected the group's advice.

"So I decided I would not go home, and I went down to Dupont Circle, and I met some people there. They said, yes, you can crash with us, and we went to this vacant apartment, and I stayed there a night. I woke up the next morning, and there were some newspapers on the floor, so I looked at them, and there was an old *Quicksilver Times* there."

It was in the newspaper that Mouse found a listing for Runaway House.

"So I called, and they said, yes, come over." The young runaway spent the next two weeks at the shelter, but, he

52

said, "Nothing got worked out." Instead, he ended up being busted by the police.

"I was arrested going back to Runaway House one night, and I was taken down to the station and booked. My father came and picked me up and took me home, and we got into a big fight. I stayed home for a week, and he said, 'Now, if you want to leave, leave. The door—once you go out the door—the door is going to be locked forever.' So I left, and I got on a bus and went to New York."

Mouse spent that summer "cruising around," as he put it. He went back to Runaway House where he "stayed for awhile." He said he had no contact with his father for six months.

Finally, Mouse broke the silence and called his father "because I had to get back into school, and I wanted to finish school." Mouse did return to school. Later, however, his father signed the needed papers and the courts placed Mouse in a foster home. This was done in order to get the necessary help for Mouse. To an extent, Mouse fulfilled a prophecy made by his parents as far back as he could remember. It was, he said, "constantly drilled into my head that I would never be anything." Communication was, by now, virtually nil between Mouse and his father. As he put it, they spoke "very, very rarely."

During Mouse's runaway "journey," he also got caught up in the world of hard drugs. These included, he said, the so-called "mind-expanding" hallucinogenic drugs. "I got really heavily involved in all types of hallucinogens, and to some extent, I got involved with heroin and cocaine," Mouse recalled.

At the Senate hearings, William Treanor, a director of Runaway House, criticized what he felt was a difference in the way runaways of different races were treated. "If you are white (pointing to Becky), you go to a mental hospital; if you are black (pointing to Mouse), you go to a reform school. But that seems to be the thrust of the whole system . . . young people pretty much can't get help until they commit some kind of a crime."

Also, Treanor continued, "the system is set up, has been set up, I believe, primarily to serve the need of the professionals involved and not the needs of the young people. A lot of Becky's difficulties stem from the fact that even after it was identified that she had such a serious family problem, nothing could be done about it because she had not stolen a car or robbed a bank or been picked up for prostitution. No one would deal with her. She had to do something more. Finally, her father agreed to pay some of the costs of her living at a group foster home."

Treanor then discussed Mouse's case in the same situation. "In Mouse's case," Treanor went on, "he had not, in effect, signed up for the services that society offers by stealing a car or sticking somebody up on the street. So what we had to do with him in order to get services for Mouse was to find a friendly police officer, and there is such a thing; find a friendly intake worker, and there are quite a few of those; find a friendly judge, and they exist also."

Treanor then outlined the strategy whereby they were able to see that Mouse was placed in a situation that was better than the one he left.

"What we did is," Treanor said, "we drew up papers on

Mouse as being beyond control. We did this ourselves. We gave them to the cop, who took them to Mouse's father, who signed them. . . . His father signed them, we took them down to the intake worker. The intake worker took them to the judge. The judge found Mouse to be incorrigible or whatever their label is. Then we had it worked out with the welfare department, and he was placed in a group foster home. But we had to go through all of that in order to get Mouse some services. We told him jokingly, 'just go out and steal a car, Mouse, so we can deal with the problem.' But that is the only way we could deal with it."

Senator Bayh replied to Treanor's description by calling it "a sad story in a society that prides itself on being compassionate. If you steal a car or stick up a corner grocery store, there are all kinds of facilities and services to help or treat you. But if you have a problem that has no criminal dimensions, we do not have the facilities necessary to treat the problem.

"That, of course," continued Bayh, "is the purpose of our bill, to try to provide those services and make them available before a child becomes stigmatized and perhaps irreversibly channeled into a life of crime."

By the summer of 1975, it was still too early to test the full impact of the 1974 runaway bill. The financing of runaway houses, for instance, was only beginning. One question still remained that was hard to answer. How many of the one million estimated runaways a year could take advantage of these centers? Although an estimated 90 or 95 per cent of the runaways do eventually return home, this still leaves about 100,000 youths a year who may become "street people."

It would be less than fair and accurate to label every single runaway as belonging to a certain group or category. But we can see, some experts say, certain patterns that indicate a runaway is a certain type. Which person ends up in which facility may depend on the type of runaway the individual is.

At the 1972 Senate hearings, for example, Dr. Helm Stierlin, a psychiatrist, presented a report entitled "Characteristics of Suburban Adolescent Runaways." In 1974 Dr. Stierlin incorporated this report into a book called *Separating Parents and Adolescents.*

Dr. Stierlin identified four major categories of runaways. These included the following: "the uncontrollable 'ne'er-do-wells,'" "the 'crisis' runaways," "the sweet 'bad' girls," and "the lonely schizoid runaways." A fifth category emerged. These were the "abortive runaways." With each type or category, the doctor presented a representative sample.

George fell into the category of the uncontrollable ne'er-do-well. By the time George ran away at the age of fourteen, he had already set a pattern of being "difficult to handle." Determined to get his own way, he would "throw tantrums" to ensure that his demands were met. "Also, from early on," Dr. Stierlin reported, "George showed a 'tough and mean' side." He took money from other children by threatening to beat them up, "stole their food, and seemed bent on mischief."

Further, George "often ran away from home, first for hours, then for half days, then for days. He ran away for several days (at 14) after he had stolen some jewelry out of his mother's jewelry chest and she had found out. He returned after he had gambled away the money and had heard his father insist over the telephone that his mother would die of a heart attack should he stay out longer," Dr. Stierlin noted.

Later, the psychiatrist recalled, George got involved with "a tough motorcycle gang," dropped out of school, and was arrested for the theft of "several thousand dollars worth of jewelry."

"George's case," concluded Dr. Stierlin, "although in some respects extreme, appears typical for the 'ne'er-do-wells' in our sample. Their running away appears tied to an impulsive life style," to avoiding "school and learning. . . ."

Runaways like George, Dr. Stierlin said, also showed a desire for "criminal delinquency, and an easy access to peers (their own age group) who also tend to be delinquents."

In his book, Dr. Stierlin also identifies George as a "casual runaway." He writes that "many successful runaways seem to experience neither qualms nor difficulties when they separate from their families. Nor do they seem blocked from moving into the runaway culture of peers. Rather than appearing agonized and (easily changed), they impress us as casual and tough."

The psychiatrist also noted that "these 'casual runaways,' or, better, 'driftaways,' easily find (if they are boys) girls who turn into willing sex partners. Yet, too, they discard these girls casually once they have used them."

A possible victim for George might be Lorraine. Dr. Stierlin called her a "crisis runaway." Until Lorraine was about fifteen, she was doing fine. "Suddenly," the doctor reported, "everything seemed to go wrong. She ran away from home overnight. Her parents were informed by the police the next morning that she had been picked up in an abandoned house together with several boys and girls who had been found with LSD and marijuana in their possession."

As a result of her escapade, Lorraine got "stern warnings from all sides — parents, police, teachers," and did, for the moment, put a halt to her running.

However, it was not too long before Lorraine got into trouble again. She took to cutting classes, became sexually involved with "several boys," and "took drugs in varying amounts." To hide her truancy, Lorraine forged passes and just plain lied to "anybody and everybody."

"Finally," Dr. Stierlin reported, "the bubble burst." Lorraine, disgusted with her life style, which by now had become a "mess," ran away from home. She fled to a "hippy commune." But her stay at the commune was very short, as Dr. Stierlin explains. "Two and a half days later her father brought her home. . . . Lorraine returned home tired, disillusioned, and ready for anything. Under these circumstances she agreed to try family therapy."

Lorraine began to make progress. She returned to school and began to get good grades again. She tried to stay out of trouble, although she occasionally did stray into sex and drugs. But her behavior did change for the better. She became active in school activities and even learned a foreign language. "So far," reported the psychiatrist, "she has not run away again." In fact, he noted, "Lorraine—immersed in studies, poetry, and college activities—seems to have mastered her crisis." (In his book, Dr. Stierlin reported that Lorraine had gone on to college.)

Lorraine differs from George in that her problems primarily "seemed to reflect a crisis that began when she was 15." By contrast, with George it was a matter of "unfolding character problems which chiefly seemed to account for the running away," the doctor reported.

If there is a female counterpart to George, it might be the sweet "bad" girls who run away—like Tracy.

"Tracy ran away from home for the first time when she was not quite 13," Dr. Stierlin reported in his study. "This happened, according to her father, after he (the father) had accidentally found and read a letter of Tracy's wherein she made 'an immoral proposition' to a boy."

When the father confronted his daughter with this information, "Tracy took off," reported the doctor. Based on the father's testimony, the doctor found that, while on the road, Tracy "did, in fact, seek the company of 'bad' older boys. . . . The father then rescued her from her bad male company and brought her home."

But the matter did not end there. Before Tracy and the family began treatment with Dr. Stierlin, "six similar runaway episodes followed." Furthermore, each such episode "appeared more ominous than the preceding one." Dr. Stierlin tells us why.

"The last three times Tracy had run away to major Eastern seaboard cities where she had found shelter with other runaways. With these she had slept around and repeatedly had 'freaked out' on bad LSD trips. Again her father had managed to rescue her each time and, again, each time this rescue had (ended up) in a brief, blissful reunion where everything was forgiven. Then the runaway cycle had begun anew, heralded by Tracy becoming more irritated, restless, and depressed."

Part of Tracy's problem had to do with the fact that she looked older than her age. This is a problem—as we'll see in the next chapter—that plagues law enforcement officials, as well as the girls themselves.

At the age of sixteen, as Dr. Stierlin tells us, "Tracy looked sweet and soft. She was in full sexual bloom and was aware of this bloom. On account of her seeming sexual maturity and a sophisticated manner of talk, she impressed people as being older than her 16 years. Her parents defined Tracy as the most sensitive of their three daughters, but also the one most hell-bent."

In his conclusion, Dr. Stierlin reported that, "In some respects these sweet 'bad' girls seemed to form the female counterpart of the all-male 'ne'er-do-well' runaways. (The ones in his study were all boys.) In other respects, though, they seemed to share (important) features with the girls in the 'crisis' runaway group. . . ."

The fourth category of runaway identified by Dr. Stierlin was the "lonely schizoid runaway." The closest example of a member of this group, said the doctor, was Roy. (A schizoid is a person suffering from schizophrenia, a serious mental illness reflecting extreme forms of misbehavior.) "Roy entered our outpatient treatment program at the age of 16, together with his parents and his younger brother Bill," Dr. Stierlin reported. "This happened (about) one year after Roy had begun to be late for school, or had skipped his

60

classes altogether." As a result, we are told, Roy's "alarmed and tense mother had arranged for Roy to see a psychiatrist twice a week. Roy, however, had shown no more enthusiasm for his (therapy) than he had shown for his school work. He had become tardy in attending his therapy sessions and eventually had rejected them altogether."

Dr. Stierlin then discusses the sessions between Roy and himself on the one hand, and Roy and the family on the other.

"In the family sessions he was mostly mute. Sometimes he had a whimsical smile on his face; more often he seemed sullen. A number of times he exploded and devastated his mother with some perceptively unfavorable comment on her behavior." Gradually, Roy began to avoid the sessions until he finally stopped going. His parents continued going a bit longer, until that, too, came to an end.

"By this time," Dr. Stierlin notes, "Roy had lost all interest in school. He spent almost all of his time alone in his room, either reading, tinkering with stereo equipment, or just staring in front of him. He refused to meet his former buddies and made no attempts to get to know girls. A few times, though, he (agreed) to receive and go out with one former classmate." This meeting of classmates led to trouble for Roy, as the doctor explains.

"After having roamed the streets with this boy one particular evening, Roy did not return home as expected. Instead, he continued to wander around in the city after his friend had left him. Finally, the night descended upon him. He wandered around until the early morning hours of the next day when he climbed on a fire escape ladder into the

5th floor apartment of a big residential building. Here he stumbled into a sleeping young woman who alerted the police."

Asked why he had taken this particular "journey," Roy smiled and replied only that, "I just had to do it. I don't know why."

Roy was subsequently placed in a mental hospital "where he has been diagnosed as schizophrenic. By now," reports Dr. Stierlin, "he has run away from this hospital at least a dozen times."

The doctor concluded that "it appears that runaway attempts in this group of lonely schizoid individuals often reflect a search for figures from the individual's fantasy lives (which may or may not resemble real life figures). Also, these attempts seem more triggered by (peculiar) clues than seems the case with runaways from the other groups which tend to run away after hassling with their families."

The last group of runaways is known as "abortive runaways." These youngsters were among those Dr. Stierlin called "runaway failures." They were not the so-called "homebound" who, despite poor conditions at home, were unable or unwilling to run away.

"One fourteen-year-old boy," Dr. Stierlin explains in his book, "repeatedly tried to run away; but only a few blocks away from his home he would loiter around a traffic crossing in such absent-minded fashion that a policeman would become concerned."

The doctor also cites the case of another abortive runaway, also fourteen years old. "After domestic hassles," she "would run angrily into a park, yet leave her bicycle in sight of neighbors who were friends of her parents."

These attempts at running away from home, concluded Dr. Stierlin, "highlighted their (the adolescents) strong, intact psychological ties to their families."

Unlike these runaways, other runaways can be said to be, to an extent, "successful." The reason they are successful, according to Dr. Stierlin, is that "they get away from their parents for longer stretches of time than the abortive runaways and . . . can find a (place) in the runaway culture of peers. And, for a while at least, they can make it on their own (providing, of course, there is spillover from society's affluence). Yet, unlike most casual runaways, they remain involved with their families, often intensely so, and finally return to the family orbit.

"While on the road, however, though still tied to the family, as if on a 'leash,' they often seem deeply conflicted—conflicted about (various things)." These conflicts include: "running away from their parents . . . living in the runaway culture . . . hurting others while pursuing their own ends. Above all, their running away reflects a crisis in their and their parents' lives," Dr. Stierlin concluded.

Sometimes that crisis involves the police.

4.

On Patrol: The Runaway Unit

"Oh, I definitely think it's getting worse. For one thing, the numbers are increasing. And I think the economic situation today is going to create a false surge that we'll have a little difficulty in dealing with. It'll be a temporary surge . . . A lot of circumstances will be created in homes that otherwise would have survived. Dad's out of work. The pressure is on. People are on each other's necks. Junior is being told to get a job when last year he was told he was going to be sent to college. So I think a great many pressures are going to evolve out of this that we perhaps are as yet unaware of. But I think we'd better be ready to deal with [this] because we're going to have an awful lot of non-criminal types floating around having to eke out an existence by some means. Legal or otherwise. One basic fact is, we've all got to eat, one way or the other."

The speaker is Police Officer Warren McGinniss. He is a member of a unique part of the New York City Police Department: the Runaway Unit.

On Patrol: The Runaway Unit

It is the job of the unit to locate and, if possible, return runaways. But the role of the Runaway Unit is best described by the men who serve within it.

The Runaway Unit was started in 1972, because, says Officer McGinniss, "there was a need. Precincts in the Village area were inundated with runaway people, not necessarily children, during this period of the sixties. You know, the Village has always been a mecca for runaways. And back in the old days, if you want to go back to Horatio Alger thinking, many came here to be artists, because the life here was always on the deliberate, permissive, free, and easy side. They could blend in, in many cases. Then came the sixties, with the social, political runaway, which had nothing to do with adventure and had nothing to do with today's runaway. That was an era by itself. They had completely different thinking, different reasoning, different attitudes, and got involved in different kinds of problems. That period began to change with the end of the sixties, and the Village became a rip-off for kids. A lot of people down here, knowingly or otherwise, took advantage of the Village. A lot of seemingly well-meaning people operated a 'crash pad.' Kids thought they were going to move in. And they found out after two or three days that not only everything they had with them goes to the pad, but they are required then to produce [support the pad]. And producing is not always that easy."

The runaway unit is located in the heart of New York City's East Village. The police officer who is speaking, a father in his own right, discussed the runaways he has met. Many, he said, were repeaters.

"Recidivism [relapse of previous condition] is commonplace. The youngster that we get that we are fortunate enough to turn around on the first appearance is the unusual. The age at the present time is a median age of around fifteen. I think by the end of this year [1975], we'll see that dropping down. If it doesn't become fourteen, it will be darn close to it. The fourteen-year-olds are very common here. I might add, our principle problem [is that] we're dealing with 10 per cent. We're dealing with the victims. The runaway who comes to town and gets smart and goes home; finds a friend and survives; gets a job; whatever— we never see. We have one sole objective. That is to be in the street in problem locations, looking for the youngster who is bewildered, who's new, who appears to be in trouble, and then finding out who, what, where, when, and why . . . and what can we do about it.

"We are not a missing persons' bureau. We are not out searching for John Doe, reported missing, although we do get parents banging on our doors and sending us photographs daily, because we have established some sort of reputation.

"Our numbers would appear to be small compared to the problem itself. I would anticipate in 1975, we would do somewhere between 1,500 and 2,000 investigations. About 500 will be identified correctly as runaways. I'm being specific there for a reason, because our laws have been changed. For instance, the age of majority for New York state is sixteen. At the age of sixteen, a youngster in New York City is free to thumb his or her nose at their parents

. . . and do whatever they please, provided they don't break any laws. If they do break any laws at that age, they come under the same authority as the general public. If you break the law, you're in trouble. . . ."

One area where P.O. McGinniss is particularly frustrated, he says, is in the victimization of children.

This is how he explained the legal situation to me, as he saw it.

"The general feeling in the streets, among street people, in New York, is that there are few rules. They have no fear of courts, no fear of police. They are generally confident that no matter what they do, they are going to beat it. Most particularly applied to the nature of the business which we most often see: the victimization of children. To get a conviction of a pimp is only a few steps away from an impossible feat. And if you did accomplish that monumental deed, the chances are about seven out of ten that you're going to be dealing with a judge that really does not understand, or because he doesn't know what it's about, cannot believe the true nature of this picture. And so you come off with a light sentence of some kind or a minimum sentence, probation, whatever."

For example, Officer McGinniss says, "How about if you have arrested a pimp that has been in bed with a fourteen or fifteen-year-old girl? And you've got the girl there admitting or making a statement to that effect, and you've caught them in the physical circumstances, and you have the testimony of the officer, and the judge's reaction could very well be, 'ahh, she's only a [prostitute].' Now, you tell me. Is she a child? Or is she a (prostitute)? And if she is a (prostitute), how did she get to be one? Who permitted that? What circumstances permitted her to be free in the street to ply her trade? To even be arrested and not identified because the numbers are so great, it's impossible to make a positive identification of everybody who passes through the system."

McGinniss also notes that this situation can sometimes lead to tragedy. "Many girls are murdered," he said. "More than we'll know. The current example," he said, "is Karen Baxter, who got arrested, released, went through the swinging doors, and came back out into the street, got murdered in a hotel room at Lexington and 26th [Street] and then turned out to be fifteen."

The problems would seem insoluble. The Runaway Unit is one way of dealing with them, however. Indeed, it may also be the only police unit of its kind involved with youths.

"Some time ago," McGinniss told me, "the police were not equipped to deal with the problem. Today we may still be the only Runaway Unit in existence in the country that is devoted solely and specifically to the problem of runaways. There may be some. To our knowledge we're the only ones who do what we do. Now other cities will tell you, we've had one for twenty years. But what you find out is that what they've had is that as soon as somebody turned up as a runaway or missing person, they got sent to a youth officer and he then took care of the processing.

"I don't know of any cases where they've had people actually out in the street, walking. We do more walking than riding. And mingling. Making friends. One of our biggest policies is establishing a rapport with street people. A group of prostitutes on a corner will not run when we approach. They know we're not going to bust them, because they know we're looking for children. We're not going to waste our time with the turnstile on prostitution. Spending all our time sitting in some place doing paper work, when some kid is out there in the street being used."

The runaway unit itself consists of some six men and a sergeant. Yet the area of their responsibility seems staggering. For example, it has been estimated that approximately 20,000 runaways hit the sidewalks of New York City each year.

"New York City's figure itself for under seventeen-year-olds in 1974 was close to 16,000," Officer McGinniss told us. "That's all types of reported runaways. We must bear in mind that there were many who were not reported missing. Many who were gone, more specifically boys, for two or three days, and then came home, but were not even recorded; they're not in the figure." Furthermore, he told us, "The Board of Education, in 1972, estimated some 200,000 'throwaways.' Now those are not runaway children. Those are children who could go home any time they felt like it, and often do drop in once or twice a week, and eat something or steal something or change clothes. [To avoid confusion, these would best be classified as 'walkaways.']

"What they are talking about," he said, "are drifting youngsters, truant from school, with little or no attention paid to that fact. The Bureau of Attendance is understaffed, underfinanced and, even if they were staffed and financed, there is little they could do legally anyway, because the ultimate they could deal with is the Family Court. And the Family Court has no recourses."

The Family Court, he said, "can just try to sift out what cases they can hope for the best, and make assignments to social agencies. . . ."

A ringing phone interrupted McGinniss. He spoke for a short time and then turned back to his visitor. He continued his discussion of his dealings with Family Court, and then talked of the Karen Baxter tragedy.

"I described to you earlier the circumstances that could prevail in the Family Court. Once in a while, we would have a judge who had nerve or the child was so obviously a child that there was no choice, and they would have to be placed in custody while we did an investigation to find out who they were. And, of course, we're assisted in that investigation by the social services. . . ."

The basic problem in the courts, as McGinniss sees it, is that a fifteen-year-old girl could be mistaken for a girl of nineteen, as with Karen. Judges, he says, are hard pressed to try and find out differently. The youth officer explained the time-consuming, complicated process involved in identifying youths—especially those who have fallen into prostitution.

"You have a large kid, a big boy—perhaps a basketball type—or as is most often the case, a female who is, by today's standards, well-developed, and you're standing before a judge. He is not too familiar with street life. Perhaps he is a very dedicated, well-meaning, certainly well-qualified person, but really not aware of what's happening to people in our streets. [Now] he is looking at a youngster who the officer is saying is somebody's child, meaning four-teen to sixteen, whatever. We work according to an Inter-state Compact. This is an agreement between states on the age. We work by the age of the state of origin. So if we have a sixteen-year-old child, it may be that that person is free in New York to do as they please, but not in New Jersey. And we go by the laws in their home state, because as a child, it is their home state that is responsible for their well being.

"Now very often, any reasonable or unreasonable excuse to drop this case from the court calendar will be accepted. Someone appears and is almost unquestioned. I remember one that was done some time ago, as a result of a mysterious phone call. Somebody called up and said, 'Oh, yes. I'm the father. Oh, yes, I know her. She was born on so-and-so.' Fine. Out."

The call, Police Officer McGinniss explained, was made from the court to someone who claimed he was the girl's father, "which is commonplace with us. And we've hurt the pimps so badly, financially, that they spend time, effort, and money, in establishing false identities for these girls. So when we pick up kids now, we pick up a whole set of credentials. Either ripped off from somebody in another state, or just created out of nothingness."

This scheme carries over, he told us, "even to the extent where they will have people who have information written down with the girl's street name or alias. And she'll come in, and give us the alias and say, 'Yes, my name is Jane Smith, and I come from Philadelphia. And my mother's in Philadelphia. Here's her phone number.'

"Now everybody in New York City knows that the Runaway Unit's first move is we're going to call momma or poppa and find out who you are. So we call. And a voice on the other end says, 'Yes, that is my daughter. Yes, she was born in 1956. Yes, my name is Jane Smith, Sr.' "

A whole procedure has to take place to "break" the false identity of the kid. "And we know this. But try to explain this to a judge in a courtroom when they're in a hurry and there are sixteen cases waiting and the judge doesn't know what the heck you're talking about in the first place. Not because there is anything wrong [with the judge]; but because this is a new and different situation.

"Well, when Karen Baxter got murdered, she brought a whole lot of light into the subject. She proclaimed for all the world to see—and be unable to deny—the fact that a fourteen-year-old or fifteen-year-old person could be accepted as nineteen; could, in fact, go through a legal process. And could, in fact, be murdered.

"And I think that the fact that Karen had been murdered only the week before contributed heavily to the fact that when we came in with a girl who we really believed was a child [she was ordered held in custody.]"

Police Officer McGinniss calls this a "Jane Doe" case, because, at the beginning, the girl would not identify herself, and no one else could identify her, either. "And we would have been more than delighted to have her pop up with a true name and a true age, so that we could release her. But she could not do that. And the name she gave, of course, was entirely false."

What made the situation even tougher, McGinniss told

me, was that there seemed to be no records on the girl. As the officer put it: "No school records. No birth records. No parents. No nothing."

The girl at that point was sent to juvenile hall. An investigation began. For a week, the police were unsuccessful. Then the case came before a Family Court judge. McGinniss explains what happened next.

"And this was a point where he was now under great pressure. He was under pressure from the Legal Aid Society. They were insisting that this is a person who says [she is] 19 and the burden of proof lies with the city. You can't just pick somebody off the street and say it's a child.

"My argument was, if this is not a child, let her simply say who she was. If she is not a child, I will not only apologize, but I'll take her where she wants to go. But since she wouldn't say that, and since I truly believe . . . that she is a child—our experience is that she is a child and if we release her we are depriving her of her right to be protected as a child. This is the way the argument went.

"The judge," McGinniss says, "made very courageous decisions. Not only that day, but subsequently a week later. He ordered photographs of the child, which was the thing that broke the case. We sent them out to major cities that had come up in conversation [with the girl]. And in one of them she was recognized, and she was identified as a fourteen-year-old child—standing there looking to all the world as a full-grown woman."

For the most part, the officer says, youngsters are identified with the assistance of the court. He said there were only one or two cases one year where they [the police] were not satisfied with the individuals who were released, although the court was satisfied. He added that there were only about five cases out of 1,000—in a one-year period—that could be classified as Jane Does.

The rest of the youths were identified. In the event that someone was classified as a runaway, the case was disposed of in a certain way. We asked Officer McGinniss to define "runaway" for us and tell us something about what happens to a runaway once he or she runs into the police.

If the youngsters are truly identified as runaways, he said, "they go into the process. That is to say that we will seek assistance for them in their home state. We will be in contact with authorities there. And we will do in-depth interviews with the youngsters to determine why they left home. And if the homes are in fact dangerous, or truly unhappy places, which could well be, we will seek some kind of placement and emergency assistance for them in their home state. This means that if they jumped out of the frying pan into the fire, we don't want to pull them out of the fire and put them back in the frying pan.

"So we're going to try to get help. And we're very hopeful that Senator Bayh's bill [will] supply the funding that will make that kind of assistance available to us so that I will be able to pick up a phone and call Milwaukee [Wisconsin] and say: 'I have a child who is in trouble.' And Milwaukee will be able to say: 'Okay. We have a runaway establishment staffed by qualified people. Not staffed by former runaways who are now experts because they ran away. . . .'"

McGinniss added that he thought houses like Runaway House in Washington, D.C., and Huckleberry House in San

74

Francisco, Ca., were qualified. "And we're looking for more of the same," he said.

"We have some here in New York," he also noted. "Covenant House, for instance. We have no serious complaints with Covenant House, but we would not place a child in Covenant House who is a dedicated runner. That is to say, someone who we have [arrested], but who is not yet ready to go home. And whom we feel will take off. But that's one extreme. In between there are many others.

"In between there are many youngsters who know about us now. They've been around and they've spoken to other kids. And when they come along and someone in the crowd says, 'Ahh, that's the Runaway Unit or that's the Youth Squad'; this kid . . . everybody disappears and one steps off the curb in front of the car. Or runs the wrong way into my arms. Okay? There's a message there.

"And a lot of face has been saved. 'I didn't give up [the kids say]. I stayed away. But the police caught me.' And, of course, if the police catch you in the game of life, that's not counting as a failure. So, those things can happen. We know this. We're not novices. And we know, here's somebody who's ready to go home.

"And the next few steps we take will be the determining factors. We'll break the ice. And we'll establish a rapport. We'll go in another room and give momma or dad some instructions. 'I don't want any nonsense over that phone. I want love over that phone.' You know, that sort of thing. Meanwhile, the other officer is saying the same thing to the kid. 'No toughness. You're caught. Get on the phone and tell your mother, "I'm sorry. I love you. I want to come home." Okay? And try to mean it.'"

"But," I asked, "what if the youngster doesn't want to go home? Or what if the parents don't want to have the child come back?"

"If the kid doesn't want to go home," Officer McGinniss answered, "we have to place the child in locked custody and have her returned by custodial means."

"Some youths do end up in jail then?" I asked.

To which McGinniss responded: "What are you calling a jail? We use Spofford Juvenile Center—the only locked detention for New York City. It is not a jail."

The runaway youth officer did agree, however, that teen-agers around the United States can, and do, end up in jail. "We've had, in fact, youngsters serve time in adult prisons here charged with a crime when they were fourteen years old."

By the way, McGinniss added, a runaway was basically someone under eighteen who spent more than one night away from home without permission. "But if we counted everybody who did that, the figures would be astronomical. So we tend to look on someone as a runaway who is away from home and is demonstrating an intention to be away from home for a period of time. They're not away from home overnight because they're mad at momma; when they run to Aunt Susie's for the weekend, to hide out. I'm talk-ing about somebody who really left home.

"We also know," he added, "that runaways are far and away the principal source of prostitutes in any large city. I can't recall meeting young prostitutes [who] weren't runaways. They may be twenty, or twenty-two, or twenty-three now. But when they started, [it] was as a runaway."

We asked how the officers of the unit meet these youths.

"Sometimes we get them begging," he told us. "Sometimes they just come in for help. Once in a great while we'll get one wandering on the street with his knapsack. He's usually fresh. And it's a good day for us, because we're there early."

"Aren't most of the runaways girls?" I wanted to know.

Police Officer McGinniss returned my question with his own question. "Are most of the runaways girls? Or is it just that we see girls and we don't see boys? And boys, of course, are not on the corners advertising their wares [that is, acting as prostitutes].

"Unless," he said, "they're into male prostitution, which exists in all too large numbers, but nothing near the girls. So [they're] just not visible. If he is going to rip off a purse, he's not going to be out on a corner waving at us. So he's not to be seen so easily."

"Where does the Runaway Unit find these people?" I asked.

Police Officer McGinniss told me this: "We get many of our boys at bus terminals and train stations. Occasionally from loitering in an area—if we happen to hear an out of town accent. A New York boy disappears in the street. He blends. As most New York kids do. Which, incidentally, has to do with our statistics. Our statistics would seem to indicate to you that everybody's a white, middle class female from out of town. . . . That's not the case.

"The New Yorkers blend in New York, number one.

Ghetto kids are not likely to be sucked into the street life in New York. They're in a street life of their own. No pimp is going to talk to a New York kid and say, 'Go to work for me.' Unless the kid is really sick, the kid is going to tell him to go take a hike. There's all that to be considered.

"So the runaways are there. But a New York runaway could be standing ten feet away, and not be visible. Because they blend. They fit. They're part of the scenery."

Before I went on an actual patrol with the Runaway Unit, we discussed in further detail the area the unit covers. New York is divided into five boroughs or counties: Manhattan (where the Village is), Queens, Brooklyn, the Bronx, and Richmond (or Staten Island). The city as a whole is home to about eight million people.

We were concerned particularly with the borough of Manhattan. For one thing, this is where the Runaway Unit is based. For another, it is the port of entry for many runaways.

Manhattan is an island. It is bounded on the east by the East River, and on the west by the Hudson River. At its furthest point south, you will hit the Atlantic Ocean. At its furthest point north, you will pass through Harlem and its predominantly black and Spanish population.

This night we would be patrolling Manhattan. We would be hitting those areas heavily populated with runaways— and some of the toughest, seediest areas in the city.

In patrolling these streets, the unit relies on its own instincts and experiences, on tips from runaways, and on information supplied by other police. They patrol Manhattan and the rest of the city, when necessary, both by car and on foot.

It is night now. Darkness has fallen upon the building that houses the Runaway Unit. If the unit is new, the building is not. Far from it. The building was built during the middle of the nineteenth century. It was used as a hospital during the Civil War to aid Union soldiers.

It is late spring. The air has begun to warm as the three of us leave the building to go on patrol. There is Warren McGinnis, his partner, Robert Lopez, and me, the author.

Ordinarily, Police Officers McGinniss and Lopez work with a third partner. But because the other officer was on vacation, I was more or less filling in as the third team member. Actually, I was there as an observer.

Lopez and McGinniss are both family men. Between them they have something like nine children. Both men are also joined by the experience they bring to the job. But the two officers are different.

McGinniss is a clean-shaven Irishman, and Lopez is a Mexican-American. Both men have a ready sense of humor that contains a mixture of compassion and the cynicism of being out on the street.

The unmarked car pulls away from the curb. We are on our way.

"If we see anything," McGinniss said, "we get out and go on foot. This allows us to have closer observation, which we have to get before we stop anybody. You can't just arbitrarily stop people on the street and say, 'You look young. Who are you?' But we do make observations and see what they're doing. What do they look like? Do they look hungry? Tired? Are they begging for money? Are they wandering aimlessly? Sleeping in the doorway? That sort of thing.

"Are they dirty? Dishevelled? Do they look like they haven't had a bath in a couple of days? Do they look like they haven't had a place to sleep?"

Then what do the officers do? I asked. Once they feel the youth is a runaway, what do they say?

"Well, we've developed what we feel is a very cool approach. We try to sort of run up and be on top of them. Most often there's three of us. And what we'll do is, one of us will make the announcement: 'Hello, dear. Hello, son. We're police officers. We are from missing persons—which we're not. But because of television, that's what they understand. If you say Runaway Unit to somebody, they say, 'Huh?' So we say we're from missing persons, the Runaway Unit," McGinniss stated. He continued.

"They look around and see two men standing on either side of them; psychologically that cuts off the possibility of a bolt and run. We haven't had a foot race or a wrestling match in months.

"We don't have to come on too hard, because most of all we're dealing with youngsters. So if we can stand there with a smile, but let them see that they're surrounded, we've already dealt with a large part of the problem.

"Then we go on to explain. 'No hassle. Don't get excited. There's no problem here. We're from the Runaway Unit. We just want to make sure you're not a runaway. That's all.'

"At this point, if the kid is a runaway and he really doesn't want to go back, he may begin to hassle us. He might say, the heck with you, I'm not going. And we'll really try the best we can to talk with him. If we can't and we have good observation and we're reasonably sure that we're making the right move, which normally we are, we'll wrap him up and toss him in the car.

"This is Washington Square Park, by the way," P.O. Mc-Ginniss' voice interrupted the squawking voice on the police radio. "In the summertime it's loaded with kids. Sometimes they'll sleep here. Sometimes they're here for want of a better place to be. It also presents special problems for us because it's loaded with young NYU [New York University] students, all of whom are wearing raggedy dungarees, and [have] unbrushed shaggy hair. . . ."

Lopez interrupts. "Hey, Warren. That kid over there with the knapsack. I'd say he's no more than fifteen. He's too young to be a college student. That guy crossing the street."

We stop the car. We are now in Greenwich Village.

"Well," says Warren, (we are now on a first name basis) "let's watch him for a few minutes . . . see where he goes."

On a summer night, Warren explained while we were waiting, "there may be up to a thousand people in this park." The officers wait until their suspect comes out of the park before approaching him, "rather than go in." They'll identify themselves as police officers.

"Absolutely . . . and it's a point we make very strongly to young people. They have an absolute right to be absolutely sure they're talking to a police officer. And not a faker. Because we have a serious problem with that in New York. . . . So the [police] department advertises in general on the radio to be sure every police officer carries an I.D. (identification) card with a picture and a shield. In our case, we tell them, if it's a detective or a plainclothes officer, you have a right to say—respectfully, don't try to make a hassle—'Officer, I'm afraid. Would you please call a uniformed officer so I can be sure?' Now any reasonable cop should do that. And I would be critical of the officer if he didn't. We certainly would. We know if a kid is giving us a hard time. If we feel it's a genuine thing, we'll say, 'No problem. You stay. We're not going to make you go anywhere. We'll call a uniformed car.'"

I then asked the officers what they say to a youth they want to take in when he asks if he is under arrest.

"We say, 'No.'"

"And what if he says, 'Do I have to go with you then?'"

"Then we say, 'Yes.'"

Warren explained. "Under the Family Court Act of the state of New York, if a police officer has reasonable grounds to think that you are a runaway, he may ask you for identification. If you refuse to, or are unable to, properly identify yourself, there are reasonable grounds for him to conclude that you are a runaway, and he is then mandated by that law to identify you and return you to your parents."

"Does he go armed when he does this?" I asked.

"Every police officer goes everywhere armed, including to bed, to the delicatessen, and to walk the dog," Warren answered.

By now, the youngster with the knapsack has entered a

church. The officers conclude that he is not a runaway. We move on.

Before long we come to that area of lower Manhattan known as the Bowery. It is a strange and often sad mixture of businesses, shops, and derelicts.

Suddenly Warren says: "I have not seen that blonde in the pink dress before. Oh, nuts! They've seen us!"

Quickly our car screeches into a U-turn. We take off after a black car. The chase is on. The car roars down the wide street.

"Try to get a look at the plates," Warren says. "If it is her, the one on the right seems awfully big. I think I made a boo-boo. No, she's in the back seat, way down low."

"Can't see . . ." Bob Lopez says.

"It could be her," Warren responds. Then, "Nah . . . all that's for nothing," Warren finally says. I manage a weak smile. "Can I start breathing again?" I ask.

"That's ordinarily more than we would do," Warren told me.

We turn around. Then we stop again. Bob has spotted some girls. He gets out and begins to walk towards them. Then, about halfway down the street, changes his mind. He turns around and comes back. They're not what he's looking for.

There are some young people on the street corner watching us. They begin a brief conversation with us.

"No. We're looking for somebody," Bob tells them. There's some small talk and kidding. "Is this the guy you called about," Bob asks, "with the glasses?"

"You see, in that situation," Warren explains, "there

wasn't too much observation. We just got a quick look. Somebody, maybe young, and she's riding off.

"I hate to tell you," Warren continued. "But there are some signs, especially where prostitutes are involved, that tell you right off that something is not right here. But we're not even going to get a chance to look at her if we don't get after her right away."

We now reach St. Mark's Place. "In the sixties," Warren noted, "this was the central location for flower children. This was *the* Village. And, as you can see now, it's quieted down considerably."

We're back in the East Village, but our patrol is not over. "You see, now over here we wouldn't be likely to find prostitutes. This is East Village; what you'll find over here still is an honest-to-goodness runaway who is either crashing with somebody or staying with friends. And we'll find them, maybe, wandering around in the street," Warren said.

We head uptown.

"Part of our thing with establishing rapport with street people is—plus the fact it's just plain humanness—we get into delivering messages from parents. Very often we'll pick somebody up and identify them. And they're at that in-between [age]. They are runaways. But they're seventeen or eighteen. Legally we can't force their return. So they're still around. We can only return them if they're under the age in their state of origin. New York is sixteen. New Jersey, seventeen," Warren said.

"But there are a lot of very young people walking around this city. Some of them have been emancipated [given the rights of adults] and they're still only sixteen or seventeen.

But their own state has given up on them, so to speak. And we'll request . . . to have the family go into court and make a new petition and have a warrant issued so we could pick the child up and return him. And they don't even want it. They call us back and say, 'No, we [don't want them].'"

"What kind of reactions do you get from parents?" I asked.

"I would have to say it runs the whole gamut from hysteria to nonchalance to being resigned to . . . 'Can you help me?'"

"Do you get some who say, 'Keep him. I don't want him'?" I asked.

"Oh, yes," Warren answered.

"Many?"

"No. But more than we'd like to get. And in a case like that we'll lay it right on them and tell them: 'We're going to contact authorities in your state and . . . [begin] a neglect proceeding against you. And we're going to ask the authorities to return the child and hold the child in custody and to investigate the matter—and if possible—to bring charges against you for neglecting the child.'"

"That usually gets them going," Bob added.

We head north.

"On the right," Warren points out, "is the hotel where Karen Baxter was murdered."

We stop. We begin talking to two young, attractive girls. They are prostitutes.

"What happened to your lip?" Warren asks.

"A trick [customer] gave it to me," one of the girls answers. "He wanted his money back, but I wasn't about to give it back. So then he pulled a gun. . . ."

The officers and girls chat some more. They're worried about my presence. Am I taking pictures of them, they want to know. Warren assures them that I am not.

"Take care, kid," he says to the girls.

We drive off again.

"You know, people don't know," Bob explains. "They see us talking to them [the prostitutes] and they get the wrong idea. Like we say, it's just the basis on which we approach these kids."

"I'll tell you," Warren says. "I wish I had a five-dollar bill for every message I've delivered to one of these kids from a parent—who calls up months later and says: 'I remember you called to check on my daughter's age. Is she still in New York? Do you see her? Is she alive? How does she look? Please tell her to call home or write us a letter.' It's pathetic. It really is.

"We have a miracle once in a while, but there is not really a heck of a lot you can do. And most of the forces in society are working against you. This girl here, we were just talking to, is from North Carolina. And she was emancipated. They gave up on her. So she's of the age now. But at the time we had her, North Carolina didn't want to be bothered taking any action because they'd already returned her three or four times. She'd been in institutions and training schools, and none of it worked. So they said, 'What the heck could we do'? So we said, you know, 'What the heck could we do'? So we made a friend out of her; the best we could do."

One of the strangest parts of being out with the unit, it seemed, was that no matter what street we traveled, there seemed to be at least one young, attractive girl selling herself. I couldn't understand it. Was I being naive? Was I being too innocent?

"No," Warren answered me. "You know what you're being? You're being the general public. Nobody could believe this is going on. . . . I'm going to be a cop nineteen years next October—and when I came back to Manhattan after fifteen years as a juvenile officer in Brooklyn—I came back over here and saw what was going on right out in the open on these streets, *I* couldn't believe it."

"Look at them," said Bob, "two well-dressed men."

"There's no shortage of 'Johns' [a 'John' is a prostitute's 'customer']," added Warren. "Every place in this city," he said. "They live in a dirty little world."

"They age very rapidly," Bob adds.

In a little while, we pass a coffee shop.

"You see them all in here," Bob pointed out, "these are all prostitutes."

"Do they know you?" I asked.

"Yeah, they all know us," Warren answered. "But I don't see any 'babies.' [Youths underage.]

"You know the one over there with the leather jacket?" Warren suddenly interrupts. "Up at the counter? Do you know her?"

"No," Bob responds.

"Why is she keeping her face away from us?" Warren asks. "She's a possible," he muses. He thinks they might return later this night to see if she is "working."

Can the officers go into a coffee shop, just like that, to talk to these girls, I want to know.

"Oh, yeah," Bob says.

"We've done it," adds Warren.

"But it's not our style," says Bob.

"We try not to because it makes a big public hassle for one thing," Warren explains. "And when we do do it, we make some careful observation—we observe for a while before we make sure we're right."

"How many Karen Baxters do you find?" I ask.

"You mean dead girls?" Warren asks in return.

"Yeah."

"Well, I suspect—I have no way of knowing for sure— but I suspect that when they're murdered, we don't know about it. They get buried somewhere. So, in my heart, I believe that more of them are murdered than anybody knows about. How many, I don't know. You get a lot of mutilations. There's one guy who brands them. He has a wire hanger twisted into his initials, heats it, and brands them."

"And yet they [the girls] keep doing it?" I ask.

"They work for him forever," Warren said.

"That's their 'man'—their 'lover'," Bob noted.

"You want to take a little walk in the terminal and have a walk on Eighth Avenue?" Warren asks me.

"You're getting the rounds tonight," Bob assures me.

The Port Authority of New York bus terminal, I am told, has about 200,000 people coming through its doors every *day*. They come from all over. Among them are some thirty to forty runaways a week picked up by Port of New York police (PONY). The police have their own headquarters in the terminal, located a few blocks from the Hudson

River, on New York's West Side.

We entered the terminal and walked past the news and candy stand, the rows of lockers, the escalator that reaches the various bus depot levels, and the ticket counters.

It's about 11 P.M. The human masses that invade during rush hour have melted down to a relatively few stragglers. We are joined by a group of noisy teenagers ("They're just probably out on the town for the evening," I'm told), a few travelers, and a drunk.

The two officers check in with the PONY police. Then we check out the waiting room. The room, with its weary commuters, separates women and children from men. The idea is, I am told, to keep unwanted intruders from bothering families who are waiting for their buses to leave.

At one seat, we spot a young girl reading a book. She looks young. But she might also be a college student.

"Give her a chance," Bob says. If the girl is still there when the men finish their rounds in the terminal, they'll approach her.

We walk around the terminal a bit longer. In contrast to the teeming streets outside—which we'll be visiting shortly —all is pretty quiet.

We return to the waiting room. This time we spot the girl by a locker. She seems to be removing some clothing. The officers move in. I stand off to the side.

They identify themselves. The girl seems startled at first. Then bewildered. She is skeptical. She doesn't believe they are police. Before she identifies herself, she wants proof.

In the distance, two uniformed police see the commotion.

They approach us. Finally, everyone identifies himself and herself. The girl *is* a college student. Nervously at first— she is obviously shaken—but then more calmly, she identifies herself. Smiles and laughter relieve the tenseness of the moment.

We move on.

Warren feels the girl acted properly and wisely. She wasn't sure the plainclothesmen were police. So she asked for identification and had other police check them out.

"We're used to hassles," Bob tells me. "We take our job seriously. Sometimes too seriously."

Bob is a fourteen-year veteran. He adds: "It's uncanny how we spot them."

We leave the terminal.

We follow Eighth Avenue north. This is the Times Square area of the city. It is the area of the dirty book stores, the massage parlors, the houses of prostitution, and the pornographic movie houses. On its streets are derelicts, pimps, prostitutes, and, mixed in with them, runaways.

We continue our walk and our patrol. Occasionally we stop, observe, and check out someone who might be a runaway. But tonight is not the night for pickups. There will be other nights. Other chances. Other runaways. They come in a seemingly endless parade into the city—and into an uncertain fate.

We head back to the car.

For me, this night will be a chapter in a book, and a memorable experience. For Bob and Warren, it will be the end of another patrol. And another moment in a combined thirty-three years of experience.

5.

The Youngest Outlaws

"It was a room less than half the size of your bedroom, which was very small. It was like one little square, you could just about fit in it. And you weren't allowed to talk to anybody. And depending on what you did, you'd be in there for like a week, two weeks. You couldn't see anybody or talk to anybody. And the only person you saw was the lady that brought your dinner and breakfast.

"When you first come in, they put you in there for two hours, while they're going through your papers and stuff. I was in there only for an hour. So it wasn't really bad, but this girl that I met there, Sally, she was in for like three weeks. She tried to break out. She was in court with me, that's where I met her.

"I wasn't treated as a person. But like a routine thing. I was just one of the other people there. I remember feeling real bad, telling them, I'm not one of them. One girl was there for assault and battery—she threw somebody down the stairs or something. But I was only there as a place to stay, until I could get transportation home. I couldn't understand why they were going through the routine with me, with examinations and things.

"I was really glad to get out . . . I was fourteen at the time."

The speaker is Vickie. I met her at one of the group homes I was visiting. Vickie had been placed in a detention facility because she had broken the law. (Running away, per se, is not illegal, but it can lead to illegal acts, such as, in Vickie's case, being truant.)

Vickie had run away from her home.

In looking back on her experience three years later, Vickie feels she didn't run. She left, yes. But she left to join the carnival.

"My girl friend lives upstate and one summer I went up to see her. And there was this carnival in town and, you know, me and my girl friend got a job and it turned my head. And we just stayed with it. I think I was thirteen at the time, but they thought we were eighteen. They didn't question [us] for working papers. I guess they just took our word for it. At one point, I remember a policeman had come in and we were stopped. . . . We weren't allowed on the grounds after midnight, you know, if we were young. But that's all they did. We couldn't work after midnight. But as far as traveling, we had no problems at all.

"We traveled up and down the east coast, including Canada. Yeah, my mother was worrying . . . I called her constantly, every day during the six months I was away. No, I didn't tell her where I was. She didn't understand why.

At that time, I didn't leave because we had problems, I just left because . . . I don't know why I left. I don't know. I just felt that it was something that I had to do. [Vickie laughs]."

As a result of Vickie's fleeing, her mother called the police and filed a missing person's report.

"She didn't know where I was, but she knew I was all right," Vickie told me. But it was another story with her school principal. Because being away from home also meant that Vickie was missing school. In short, Vickie now had two legal strikes against her: she was a runaway, and she was a truant. Her principal filed a complaint.

By this time the carnival was in Maryland, and Vickie had had her fill. It was time for her to go home and finish school. She called her mother. She picks up the story from there.

"When I called my mother, I just couldn't come home. She had to call the police and tell them where I was, so they called the police in Maryland and had them pick me up. I was staying with this girl, but they couldn't leave me there; they were afraid I was going to leave again. So they had to place me in this home for a few days until I could get transportation home. And it was disgusting. We had little rooms with bars on the doors and the windows. It was like a prison. It was horrible. And if you did something wrong, they locked you in solitary." (This is described at the beginning of this chapter.)

Therefore, even though Vickie had called her mother, and told her where she was, and told her she was coming home, her mother had to notify the police in the state where Vickie lived, New Jersey.

"She had to call and tell them, because they were looking for me," Vickie explained. But, "I don't know why they had to go through the trouble of calling Maryland and tell them to pick me up. I never knew why. Because I was going home.

"Anyway, one day I was going out to lunch with my friend. When I opened the door I heard someone call my name. When I turned around I saw this policewoman there. I knew it was a policelady. She was a regular person, but she had boots on. I had a feeling, I guess. Anyway, she said, 'I have orders to pick you up.' Can you believe it? She wanted to handcuff me. And there were at least six policemen waiting outside. And I said: 'This is ridiculous.' I refused to go with her. I said: 'I'm not going to put handcuffs on.' So she said, all right, but she held my arm. And we walked out together. I thought it was pretty stupid. They said they couldn't take any chances. They were afraid that I was going to go away again, which was dumb, because I was the one that called and said I was coming home in the first place. Anyway, I went back to school and that was it."

But that was not quite the end of Vickie's tale.

When she came home, Vickie had to go to court. The judge put her on probation and released her in her mother's custody.

"I was told," Vickie recalled, "that I wouldn't have to see a probation officer, but that if I got in trouble for the next six months, I would probably be put away . . . like in a state home or something."

Although Vickie was to run away from home again, and this time not to seek the carnival, her story had a happy ending. She returned home and finished high school. (We'll meet Vickie later on again, and speak with her mother.)

Young people like Vickie are called "status offenders."

At its very basic level, a status offender is a girl or boy who commits a *status offense*. A status offense is an act that adults may commit, but that is forbidden to children. Running away is a status offense. So is truancy. Sometimes one leads to the other.

Vickie was a lucky status offender. Status offenders have little or no protection compared to adults or juvenile delinquents. Many status offenders end up in jail or some other kind of institution, such as a mental institution. Status offenders may also be known as PINS (Persons In Need of Supervision), CHINS (Children In Need of Supervision), JINS (Juveniles In Need of Supervision), or MINS (Minors In Need of Supervision).

John Rector, Sen. Birch Bayh's chief counsel, told me the following:

"A substantial portion of the young people who are not just processed by the juvenile courts, but are adjudicated [judged] and found delinquent . . . and, in fact, oftentimes housed . . . in institutions that aren't better than most . . . [prisons] are young people who haven't committed acts that would be criminal if they were [done] by adults."

According to a recent report by the National Council on Crime and Delinquency (NCCD), "of the one million youngsters under 18 who will become involved with the nation's 2,600 juvenile courts this year, 600,000 will be held in secure detention pending court hearings. 100,000 will be committed to correctional institutions for indeterminate periods."

NCCD also said that "23 per cent of the boys and 70 per cent of the girls held in juvenile institutions will be guilty of no crime for which an adult would be prosecuted."

In 1973, according to the U.S. Law Enforcement Assistance Administration (LEAA), one-third (33%) of the boys and three-fourths (75%) of the girls detained were status offenders. This was based on a survey of 60,000 youths in 722 institutions. Furthermore, the NCCD noted, "the average detention period of institutionally-committed juveniles is 9.9 months. Those held for 'status offenses' remain an average of four to five months longer than children convicted of criminal offenses."

The problem surrounding status offenders or PINS youths is that the laws they are said to be violating are often vague. This confuses an already complicated legal subject that can only be touched upon here.

The New York State Family Court Act (1962) is said to be typical of other state laws in the way in which it defines PINS. A PINS youth, it says, is a youth under sixteen "who is incorrigible, ungovernable or habitually disobedient and beyond the control of [his] parent or other lawful authority."

Because a runaway is a youth who is below the legal age to be on his/her own, and has left without parents' permission for an extended period of time, it stands to reason that a runaway falls into this category.

In New York City, most PINS youths are brought before

the juvenile justice system by their parents. This was explained by Eleanor Muhlmeyer of that city's Department of Probation. She gave some examples of what parents complained about. "The child is not getting along at home; he's truant from school; he's running away from home; he's coming home late; he may be drinking—whatever. But it's generally a complaint that's brought by the parent," she told me.

"But the juvenile justice system in the state of New York is set up through our New York State Family Court law," she added. "And it provides for an intake service initially which screens all the cases that presumably would be coming through the court system. Now intake's primary responsibility is to divert youth. . . ." Intake decides whether or not a case should be handled by the Juvenile Court. For example, intake may "adjust" the case by referring the youth and the family "to a community resource for treatment purposes. Of course," Ms. Muhlmeyer added, "this kind of planning becomes very difficult because the community resources available within the city of New York are seriously lacking. I mean, I'm sure you've come across this problem in your research."

On the other hand, sometimes the case must be sent before the court. At that point, probation steps out of the picture (and doesn't return until the judge has made a finding that this is a person in need of supervision, or that this is a juvenile delinquent).

At this point, in all likelihood, the Legal Aid Society steps in. "We represent 90 per cent of the children who come into the Family Courts of New York City," Charles

Schinitsky, director of the Legal Aid Office of Juvenile Services, told me.

The children his lawyers represent, he said, "are the poor kids. The court is a poor-kid court." They deal, he said, "with 17,000 kids a year, including the neglected, PINS, delinquents, and others. Status offenders make up between 30 and 35 per cent."

I have focused on New York for a particular reason. As Mr. Schinitsky explained it on the morning we met, "We [New York] were the first state to legislate representation on a uniform, consistent basis and called for a set of law guardians . . . lawyers in those courts to represent them [youngsters].

"We came into existence with the advent of the new Family Court in 1962. Prior to that time, in 1960, we had what was known as the old Children's Court. And this is a court that had pursued the *parens patriae* doctrine since the turn of the century. [Generally, this meant the state was acting as a parent.]

"And since it was felt that this was a civil court—it was a court out to help youngsters—there was no need for lawyers. And there was no need for technicalities that one associated with lawyers. So that, in 93 per cent of the cases, lawyers did not appear. There was no provision for counsel, since it was a civil court. The proceedings were closed to the public. In order, so they said, to protect the youngsters from publicity.

"Well," the soft-spoken, distinguished-looking lawyer continued, "in the late '50s, there began to be some concern by . . . interested children's groups . . . as to what was going on

98

in that court. There would be some feedback coming out of it indicating that many times children were being sent away when they shouldn't be sent away; also, when they *hadn't done anything.* The law itself, or the acts . . . were so broad and so vague that almost any kid could be pulled into it at any time. The PINS youngster was then called a juvenile delinquent. . . . He was the youngster who did anything which might be injurious to his general welfare and health. . . ."

By 1962, with the help of the Legal Aid Society and the state legislature, the Family Court Act became law.

"Finally," Mr. Schinitsky recalled, "they came up with some real radical innovations in the field of children's courts and juvenile courts." For example, the Act "mandated the right of counsel . . . where the youngster could not afford counsel. It also gave the youngster the right to remain silent, which was also unheard of. Because under the old doctrine, the court could talk to the child any time . . . then pull him into the court process."

At the same time, Mr. Schinitsky added, "they asked the Legal Aid Society to provide the representation. And they created a category known as PINS, separating the youngster from the juvenile delinquent." (Delinquents in New York are youths under sixteen who commit acts that would be crimes if they were done by adults. The court also has jurisdiction over neglected youths, people whose parents failed to provide for them.)

But what was taking place in New York at the beginning of the 1960s was apparently more the exception than the rule. To some extent, particularly with regard to status offenders, this has remained true through the present time.

Recently a survey was conducted for the U.S. government. The survey was unique in that it covered areas of concern to runaways—including laws.

The study is called *The Legal Status of Runaway Children.* It was conducted by Herbert Wilton Beaser and the Educational Systems Corporation. It was done at the request of, and with funds supplied by, the Office of Youth Development, Office of Human Development, of the Department of Health, Education, and Welfare.

Mr. Beaser's group was concerned with the major laws, the highest court decisions, and the opinions of attorney generals in fifty-four jurisdictions. These jurisdictions covered the fifty states, the District of Columbia, Guam, Puerto Rico, and the Virgin Isands. These laws and opinions were studied as they related to "the legal problems of major import likely to be encountered by children 'on the run'— whether running interstate or intrastate."

The summary report notes that, "the runaway child presents a peculiar phenomenon within the juvenile justice system. Statutes regarding their behavior are vague and vary widely from state to state. In 24 of the 54 subject jurisdictions, peace officers may take into custody and detain juveniles suspected of being runaways. Such runaways are variously categorized as delinquents, persons in need of supervision [PINS], or children in need of supervision [CHINS]."

It might be interesting to briefly look at the background behind the laws that deal with minors, as documented in the report. "Historically, children below the age of 21 had little, if any, control over the direction and circumstances of their lives. Common-law provisions for reciprocal rights and duties between parents and their minor children (said) that parents had the legal right to the physical care, custody and control of those children. . . ."

Parents also "had the right to provide and supervise their [children's] education, religious control and general upbringing, including discipline . . . and could retain the services and earnings of these minor offspring. . . ."

While it may not have been spelled out directly, on the other hand, there "was the implied obligation of parents to in fact provide their children with the necessities of life." Both rights and obligations ended when the child turned twenty-one.

The report also notes that the common law worked more to the disadvantage of the minor than the advantage. "Under its mantle, the minor could not give valid consent to medical, surgical or psychiatric care. If between the ages of seven and 14 and charged with . . . a crime, he or she could be tried and convicted as an adult."

Furthermore, the "minor child had no right to his or her earnings, or to a choice of [home] other than that of the parent of record. Yet he or she could consent to marriage at the age of seven!"

Also, under common law, "the unemancipated [not legally free to live on their own] minor could neither sue nor be sued, and could disavow most contracts to which he or she had been a party. There was no common-law requirement that a child attend school to fulfill the parental obligation that he or she be educated."

The report *does* note that there have been many changes in law since those days. Children have more rights today than they did years ago. For example, the report cites the fact that forty-one of the fifty-four jurisdictions have lowered the age of majority to eighteen.

But, it also explains that "in many cases, newly enacted [laws] simply imposed additional restrictions and limitations upon unemancipated minors."

For the runaway, the report says, common law and statutes [written law] "combine to create a . . . jungle that the typical runaway is ill-prepared to confront. Youngsters who have chosen or been forced to flee their homes are generally significantly younger than any established age of automatic emancipation. . . ."

If the laws that affect runaways create a "jungle" for the unwary youngster, there is, it is said, one "animal" he or she should be concerned with: the juvenile court. The juvenile court has been described as being somewhere in between a friendly, helpful facility and a hostile and dangerous place.

The debate that has been going on for years over the merits and demerits of the juvenile court system—especially concerning status offenders (including runaways)—continues at the present time.

The pros and cons of the juvenile justice system in general—and the juvenile court in particular—*as it affects status offenders* are best illustrated by persons on both sides of the bench. The children and their lawyers on one side; probation officers and judges on the other.

Parents and police, among others, also have their own

roles to play in this complicated drama of human emotions.

Perhaps we can clear up the murky legal waters a bit by looking once again into the past at the origins of the juvenile court system. Back we go to the Beaser-ESC study.

"The concept of a juvenile court," the study says, "originated early in this century as a well-intentioned attempt to shield children from the stigma of being called into the adult 'criminal' court. The privacy that would 'protect' these errant minors excluded lawyers, juries, most witnesses, the press and the public from the courtroom; the judge and the probation officer would do what was in the 'best interests' of the child."

Children's rights at that point were virtually unheard of. In fact, it's only since the 1960s that the concept of children's rights, in law, took hold—and produced results.

Up until then, in the words of one lawyer, a youngster was treated as "a piece of baggage," to be moved around from one place to another. Even today, critics of the juvenile justice system complain that the youth is still "baggage."

For example, the Legal Aid Society's Charles Schinitsky told me that they have filed a suit in a federal court against the treatment youths have allegedly received in New York training schools. The suit challenged the constitutionality of the use against youths of "solitary confinement and . . . physical restraint by means of handcuffs and other similar restraining devices."

In another federal suit, the society questioned the "indiscriminate use of Thorazine [a strong tranquilizer]." (I was later told that a court had placed limits on the time

103

a young person could be in solitary confinement. As a result of another suit, an "ombudsman" was picked to guard the rights of youths held in Spofford.)

Until a recent court decision in New York, there were no separate training schools for PINS youths and delinquent youths. In other areas of the country, meanwhile, there was no such distinction. PINS youths and juvenile delinquents were placed in the same institutions. In some states, in fact, there is no distinction between the two in law. Status offenders (PINS) are considered in the same way as are juvenile delinquents.

To an extent, this may work to the status offender's benefit, strangely enough. For example, the landmark case for juveniles is the U.S. Supreme Court decision of 1967 known as *In re Gault*. The decision mandated the right of counsel to juveniles. The Court also said a juvenile had a right to be presented with a written notice of the charges against him or her. Also, the juvenile now had a right to remain silent, and he or she had the right to face and question the accusers. A later High Court case extended the rights of juveniles still further. The evidence against them had to present a case beyond reasonable doubt: *In re Winship* (1970).

The wording of the High Court's decision in the *Gault* case is significant here. The Court found that "the due process clause of the Fourteenth Amendment requires that in respect to proceedings to determine delinquency which may result in commitment to an institution in which the juvenile's freedom is curtailed, the child and his parent must be notified of the child's right to be represented by counsel retained by them or, if they are unable to afford counsel, that counsel will be appointed to represent the child." The key words in this legalistic phrase are the concepts of "curtailed freedom" and "delinquency." In other words, if the youth faces a chance of losing his freedom by being judged delinquent, then the normal adult protections apply, such as right to counsel.

However, the Court did not specifically say whether or not status offenders were entitled to counsel (although they also frequently lose their freedom). It has been left up to the states and localities to decide whether or not status offenders are entitled to the same protections as delinquents.

Why didn't the Court say whether status offenders were entitled to counsel? I asked Flora Rothman of the National Council of Jewish Women. Ms. Rothman has served on a task force on juvenile justice appointed by the president of the United States.

"Because," she answered, "the decision did not refer to that group. Now in many states they do have that, and in New York, a PINS child will . . . get representation. But this is not something that has to be done."

Nor has the full impact of the Court's decision apparently made itself felt in the country. The Beaser-ESC study reported that the impact of such decisions "on actual juvenile-court proceedings is difficult to determine."

Such decisions, it would seem, must be taken into account in the ultimate debate: should status offenders (such as runaways) be subject to the authority of the juvenile court system?

Evidently, it is the policy of the U.S. government to answer "no." That was, in effect, what Ed Farley of the Office of Youth Development (at HEW) stated. HEW is responsible for implementing the Runaway Youth Act, which is Title 3 of the "Juvenile Justice and Delinquency Prevention Act of 1974." The rest of the act is administered by the Law Enforcement Assistance Administration.

"The official stance of this office," he said, "is that status offenses should not be handled by the juvenile justice system. It [status offenses] should not be against the law. . . ."

"One of the major thrusts of the Juvenile Justice Act," John Rector, Senator Bayh's chief counsel, stated, "was to help deinstitutionalize and decriminalize the treatment of status offenders." The act, therefore, through the use of federal funds, aims at encouraging states to treat status offenders differently "from young persons who have engaged in conduct that would be criminal if they were of majority age and truly [threatens] person and property in the community," Mr. Rector explained.

But the youthful attorney is also quick to add that the new law "did not go to the jurisdictional issue. In other words, our bill was silent on whether or not the juvenile courts should retain jurisdiction on status offenders. . . . The best we could do in that regard is to provide a moral code, and say to the states, 'Well, folks, this is the way we would advise is the best way to operate.'"

The issue, the Senate aide told me, is "really a mixed bag. In some communities it would be disastrous if you separated out status offenders from [the] juvenile court because there would be no services at all."

A number of judges, despite their own apparent misgivings about the system, would seem to agree with this view. One such judge is Joseph Williams, Administrative Judge for the Family Court in New York City.

"Many of these youngsters," Judge Williams stated, "don't belong in the juvenile justice system—though they often end up in the juvenile justice system because we have not adequately recognized and provided services for dealing with this."

Eleanor Muhlmeyer adds that "for the last couple of years, there's been a great effort by a number of factions in society to remove those status offenders from under the auspices of the court. In other words, take the PINS category out altogether. I don't know that they've come up with any plan of how to *deal* with these children, or what they will use in place of the court system. But it is their feeling the child does not belong in . . . for these kinds of status offenses. . . . And simply to say that you're going to use community resources or that you're going to help a variety of communities develop resources for treatment is kind of crazy. I mean, we don't have the resources to deal with these children. . . ."

However, the "best interests" approach of the juvenile court has, in the minds of many, done more harm than good. Reports the Beaser-ESC study: "In spite of the noble motives of its creators, the juvenile court has often rendered . . . injustices on children before it, as well as on their parents."

To put it another way, as Phyllis Ross of the National Council of Jewish Women stated: "The quarrel is basically between the due-process people and the discretion people." It is a fight, says Ms. Ross, between those who say, "How

107

are we going to protect and take care of the child?" and those who say, "How are we going to protect the child from us?" However, Ms. Ross added, "It doesn't have to be an either/or kind of thing."

The debate goes on. Beyond the subject of status offense itself, the juvenile is also concerned with other laws that cover him or her. These are laws which, although they are again meant to protect young people, often work against them.

The Beaser-ESC study, for example, noted in its 410-page report that "both statutory and common law as they exist today throughout the country are not of much assistance to the unemancipated runaway child. As a matter of fact it can safely be said that, on the whole, the law is more a hindrance than a help to such a child. The legal status of an unemancipated runaway child in the United States today is both confused and confusing. . . ."

The report cited the following example. "[I]n many jurisdictions a police officer is by statute authorized, without a warrant, to take a suspected runaway child into custody and place such a child in a detention or shelter-care home *even* where the act of running away from home is not specifically made a delinquent act or a status offense by the juvenile court statutes of that jurisdiction!"

The idea here, Mr. Beaser explains, is that some authorities think "there is something 'wrong' with the unemancipated runaway child who leaves home without parental permission," regardless of the merits of the case.

He says the thinking persists despite "the known fact that in many cases it might have been more prudent from the standpoint of the child's best interests for the child to have 'run' than to have stayed."

Furthermore, the summary of the study notes that "much can be gained by considering the strictures that legally prevent a runaway from seeking medical care, from supporting himself or herself, from attending school in a jurisdiction other than that of the parent or guardian, and, in many instances, from retaining his or her very freedom."

For example, Mr. Beaser says that "in many jurisdictions, a runaway child would find it very difficult to obtain medical care because of the child's inability to give effective legal consent to the provision of such care."

Finally, among the recommendations the Beaser-ESC report makes, is "extensive revisions" of the Interstate Compact, under which juveniles are sent home. The revisions are needed, the report says, "to make it a more effective legal instrument to solve the many legal, social and practical problems of runaway children and their parents and to protect their rights."

Once again we meet a situation where the purpose of a law or act is to be in the "best interest" of the child. The aim of the compact is to "provide for the welfare and protection of juveniles and the public."

Under the compact, the person or agency having legal custody of a child who has run away without permission may petition the "appropriate court" in their state asking for a "requisition" for the return of the runaway.

Further, under the pact's provisions, "the juvenile may be held in detention for a period of 90 days while it is determined whether the state of residence will transmit the necessary requisition for the child's return.

"At a time when the trend is to do away with detention care for status offenders, three months seems . . . long . . . to confine a child in detention while the creaky wheels of justice slowly seek to determine if the child should be returned to the child's parents or guardian," says the report.

Perhaps the most graphic account of how the law operates—or is thought to operate—was given to me by a young runaway. Frank was on the road hitchhiking with a girl friend. He said, "Like the friend I was with, she got raped . . . and it was really bad. And she didn't want to get herself in trouble. She couldn't turn around and go to the police, because we were breaking the law ourselves, too . . . My first reaction was: 'Should I call the Highway Patrol?' Then I thought: Wow! We're both outlaws. What can we do?"

What they did do, Frank said, was continue traveling with the driver who had, Frank said, raped his female companion. Flabbergasted, I asked the young runaway how the two people could continue to travel with a person like that.

Among Frank's reasons was this one: "Because it seems like when you're on the road you take rides with whatever you can get cause you don't want to take the chance of getting busted. . . ."

6.

From Huckleberry Finn to Huckleberry House

In recent years the subject of runaways has become a matter of some national concern and a good deal of media interest. Laws have been enacted; millions of dollars have been spent; and countless stories have appeared in magazines, newspapers, and books.

Yet the idea of runaways is older than America itself. Indeed, in a sense, runaways helped found the United States. Benjamin Franklin was a runaway, for example. And weren't the Pilgrim Fathers runaways? Certainly they fled a particular situation to seek a new and, hopefully, better life. And so did the millions who followed them throughout our history.

As for the fictional side of American history, we have Mark Twain's Huckleberry Finn, who captured the imagination of millions of American youngsters—and adults, as well.

Therefore since runaways are nothing new to this country, why all the sudden fuss?

Part of the answer lies in the growth of American society in terms of population and the mass media. An event such as the Houston slayings in the summer of 1973 had an instant impact. It spawned national concern for runaways in the form of hot lines, runaway houses, crisis centers, and legislation.

Furthermore, the development of the American economy, the settling of the frontier, the passage of child welfare legislation, and the restructuring of the American family all have had their impact on American society.

We have already seen in other chapters, for example, how an American economy in the throes of inflation and recession worsened tensions in families. The result: thousands upon thousands of "throwaway" children.

Rising divorce rates have also taken their toll of young victims. Most of the youngsters I spoke with came from broken homes. Either one parent was missing or the marriage had disintegrated long before any court could make its dissolution legal.

Dr. Margaret Mead, the noted anthropologist, has studied the family, children, and youth for fifty years. In 1973 Dr. Mead told a Senate subcommittee that, "Our families are in disarray, our whole system of help for family and children is being aggressively dismantled." The famed scientist added: "We have more and more broken families, more and more poor fathers who cannot support their children, more and more children who have no one to care for them.

"It is estimated now that we have about 3 million doorstep children. These are teenagers, young people for whom you cannot find any person who can give permission for them to have their tonsils out, who are living without any responsible care by society. Many runaways are a small section of this group," Dr. Mead said.

The hearings Dr. Mead spoke at were held by Senator Walter Mondale's Subcommittee on Children and Youth. The subject: American Families: Trends and Pressures: 1973.

Dr. Mead's words were reinforced by Dr. Urie Bronfenbrenner, another noted family authority. "The most important fact about the American family today," he said, "is the fact of rapid and radical change. The American family is significantly different from what it was only a quarter of a century ago."

Then he added the following examples.

"Fifty years ago in the state of Massachusetts 50 per cent of the households included at least one other adult besides the parent. Today the figure is only 4 per cent.

"The divorce rate among families with children has been rising substantially during the last 20 years. The percentage of children from divorced families is almost double what it was a decade ago. If present rates continue, one child in six will lose a parent through divorce by the time he is 18." Twenty years ago, that figure was one in twelve.

A White House Conference on Children once reported that, "In our modern way of life, it is not only parents of whom children are deprived, it is people in general. A

113

host of factors conspire to isolate children from the rest of society." Among these factors were the following:

the fragmentation of the extended family
the separation of residential and business areas
the disappearance of neighborhoods
occupational mobility
child labor laws
the abolishment of the apprenticeship system
television

The 1970 White House Conference on Children spelled out some of these factors in greater detail. It noted that "in today's world parents find themselves at the mercy of a society which imposes pressures and priorities that allow neither time nor place for meaningful activities and relations between children and adults. . . . [These] downgrade the role of parents and the functions of parenthood, and . . . prevent the parent from doing things he wants to do as a guide, friend, and companion to his children. . . ."

The report points out that "the frustrations are greatest for the family of poverty where the capacity for human response is crippled by hunger, cold, filth, sickness, and despair. For families who can get along, the rats are gone, but the rat-race remains. The demands of a job, or often two jobs, that claim mealtimes, evenings, and weekends as well as days . . . the trips and moves necessary to get ahead or simply hold one's own . . . the ever increasing time spent in commuting, parties, evenings out, social and community obligations . . . produce a situation in which a child often

spends more time with a passive babysitter than a partici-
pating parent."

The end result of all this is a much-used word: alienation.
It shows itself in action through some alarming statistics.
This alienation, Dr. Bronfenbrenner indicated, "is reflected
in the rising rates of youthful runaways, school dropouts,
drug abuse, suicide, delinquency, vandalism, and vio-
lence. . . ."

He then cited the following figures:

> the proportion of youngsters between the ages of 10
> and 18 arrested for drug abuse doubled between 1964
> and 1968;
>
> since 1963, juvenile delinquency has been increasing
> at a faster rate than the juvenile population;
>
> over half the crimes involve vandalism, theft, or
> breaking and entering;
>
> and, if the present trends continue, 1 out of every 9
> youngsters will appear in juvenile court before age 18.

Furthermore, Dr. Bronfenbrenner noted, "These figures
index only detected and prosecuted offenses." (Flora Rothman of the National Council of Jewish Women states that
"half of police contacts with kids end in arrests." In other
words, she said, "Two million kids a year are arrested.")

Young people who run away may be part of a larger
"runaway group." For example, recalled Dr. Bronfenbrenner, "the growing number of divorces is now accompanied
by a new phenomenon: the unwillingness of either parent
to take custody of the child. And in more and more fam-

ilies, the woman is fleeing without waiting for the mechanism of a legal or even agreed upon separation." The result, therefore, is "runaway wives"; again not a new factor in American history, but evidently a newly disturbing one.

In some cases, "runaway wives" may be the result of increased pressures when they are the heads—sole heads—of the family. The rise of the number of "father-absent homes," notes Dr. Bronfenbrenner, places "increasingly greater responsibility . . . on the young mother."

In any case, they may be considered a part of what one expert has called "a runaway culture." This concept was described in Dr. Helm Stierlin's book.

Dr. Stierlin identified this "runaway culture" among both youth and middle-aged parents. "These parents, too," Dr. Stierlin wrote, "may feel tempted to move away or run away from jobs and family relations which, they believe, only mire them in stalemates and hassles. They, too, may desperately wish to make new starts in life and, like their adolescent children, may strongly feel the lure of a 'runaway culture.'"

One example of this is a runaway with whom I spoke. One day her stepmother decided she didn't want to stay any longer. So she picked herself up and left. Some months later, the girl's father took off after her stepmother. As a result, the girl and her sisters were left to fend for themselves until neighbors took over and called the authorities. The father and his wife haven't been heard from since. And the three children have all been separated; split up among various foster homes. The youngest is fourteen. Some foster homes can be brutal too. The children may be treated cruelly—both physically and mentally. In addition, although foster care is supposed to be temporary care, oftentimes it isn't. Children may end up living in foster homes permanently.

Sid Johnson, a staff member of Senator Mondale's subcommittee, expanded on this one morning.

"Forty percent of the kids in foster care," Mr. Johnson stated, "go there because of the hospitalization of the mother, either mental or physical. Our way of responding in this country is foster care, which we consider to be a temporary placement until everything else works out. But by and large, it's not a temporary placement. It's a permanent placement. Very few of the children who enter foster care ever get returned to their families." And the foster care system, he went on, "is almost exclusively through court placement or initiated by the . . . parent."

One result of this, by the way, was legislation in New York aimed at getting children out of foster care and into adopted families. State Senator Joseph Pisani, an upstate Republican, called the law he sponsored, "the kind of legislation that will help to minimize the risk of trapping children unnecessarily in the limbo world of foster care." (Congress too has expressed concern over alleged abuses in child care through hearings.)

Beginning in the sixties, in response to a growing need of where to place troubled youths, scores of runaway houses, crisis centers, drop-in centers, group foster homes, and free clinics began to mushroom across the United States. These were alternative settings—alternative to the standard, institutional outlets for youngsters in trouble, ranging from training schools to child care agencies.

Most of these places had similar problems getting started. Hassles with the police, the "establishment," and the community were among the difficulties these agencies faced.

My research for this book took me from New York's Covenant House to San Francisco's Huckleberry House to Washington, D.C.'s Runaway House and, finally, to the Teaneck Home for Girls in Teaneck, New Jersey. I spoke with counselors, volunteers, staff, and, of course, the young people themselves.

These houses share a common development. They started outside the mainstream of standard child care agencies. Gradually, they have expanded to provide more than just a hot meal and bed and counsel. They have developed a full range of services for runaway youths.

A case in point is Covenant House in New York's East Village. "Covenant House," director Father Bruce Ritter said, "runs the oldest continuing crash pad in the history of the city."

Covenant House, he said, got started as "kind of an accident. My background is academic . . . But, in 1968, I asked my superiors if I could move off campus and work more directly with the poor here in New York City. And they agreed. So I moved down to the East Village. And I found a couple of adjoining apartments there in a tenement. I guess both apartments were as big as half this room. . . ."

But the apartments weren't so small that thieves couldn't find them comfortable. They took nearly "everything. Money, clothes, furniture, television; they even took my black suit and collar. But junkies had infested the area."

"You see," explained Fr. Ritter, dressed casually in shirt and slacks, "the East Village in early '68, late '67, like Haight-Ashbury, had become sort of a mecca for the flower children. . . . Very quickly, both Haight-Ashbury and the East Village were taken over by hard drugs. And the flower culture got drowned; smashed out flat—and a lot of kids were stranded there on the reefs.

"One night, in the winter of '68, at 2 o'clock in the morning, six kids knocked on my door; four boys and two girls. All of them under sixteen. . . . And they asked if they could sleep on the floor of my apartment. And I said yes, and gave them some food and blankets. And they slept there, curled up in a row like so many ten pins.

"And the next morning it was cold and snowy outside, and it got kind of awkward. They didn't want to go away." The girls volunteered to do the dishes and the boys began cleaning up the rest of the place. "And one kid went outside and brought back four more kids and said, 'This is the rest of our family.'

"I asked them where they had been living. And they told me, in one of the abandoned buildings down the block. But they had been burned out by junkies because they didn't want to do what the junkies had wanted them to do. Specifically, they wanted the kids to go out and steal. And, you know, sex was just part of all that stuff. And these ten kids had been exploited by a friendly couple upstate who took them in for a couple of days, but as a price, they had to star in pornographic movies, which they did.

"The ten were traveling—all runaways—as a 'family';

it was a fluctuating membership. They had been together for two or three months, which is a long time in the life of one of those families. The average crash pad in 68-69 never lasted more than three months.

"I had those kids and didn't know what to do with them. So I began calling child care agencies all over the city and got turned down. They weren't on the city bill. They didn't have psychosocial histories. They didn't have referral status. No social worker was worrying about them. The family court didn't assign them anywhere; they weren't reimbursing the kids."

"Wasn't anybody looking for them?" I asked.

"The advice I got summed it all up pretty succinctly," he answered.

"The head of one of the major child care institutions in this city . . . said, 'Father, have the kids arrested.' And I said, 'Why? What crime did they commit?' And he said: 'It is a crime to be 15 years old and homeless in New York City.' And it is."

But, "I didn't have them arrested, and I didn't have the guts to kick them out. So I kept them." Thus Covenant House was born.

They "never had any money, were always broke. I was never really sure we were going to be able to pay the rent. But, you know, hundreds of kids began coming to us— word of mouth—and the cops were upset—you're not supposed to take care of kids without a license. A priest isn't supposed to be living down in one of those tenements; you're supposed to be in a rectory . . . or teach—but that didn't stop the kids. And I really didn't have intentions,

120

I guess, of starting a child care agency. . . ."

Eventually, in 1972, Father Ritter found that wall-to-wall youths were beginning to take their toll on his own life. He moved out of the apartment. But still the boys and girls came.

"So we just had to go and become a licensed child care agency. And we had a very ambivalent position in this city. The judges in the family court were sending us kids; the Bureau of Child Welfare was sending us kids; kids were sending us kids — the police didn't like *any* of it.

"And the Bureau of Child Welfare would say, 'What are we going to do with that priest?' Although they kept sending us their hard-to-place kids — apologizing that, well, we can't pay you, of course, because you're not on the city bill, because you're not an agency. But thank you for taking care of the kids, for giving them a place to stay, and all that."

Father Ritter also had "lots of hassles with the kids who need medical help. In the beginning, when I had to take a kid to [the hospital] who needed help, sometimes really bad, they would say, 'Well, we can't touch him because we've got to contact his parents.' Well, pretty quick, I would sign them in as my own children. It got to be a joke after a while. I was bringing them black kids. . . . But they didn't care as long as they had a signature."

But the constant hassles—being in debt, the overcrowding in tiny apartments, the toilet in the hallway or the kitchen— got to be too much.. With the help of friends from the college where Fr. Ritter had been teaching and other volunteers, a decision was finally made.

"We just had to get organized or die. We couldn't survive. So . . . we wound up in October of '72 with a charter, licensing us to take care of kids. We had to charter all the responsibilities; the obligations to have social services: social workers, doctors, psychologists. . . . All we had were hundreds of kids coming to us and no money and no houses, and a charter. So I began to speculate. . . . I leased buildings on instinct and promises.

"I never had any money. We still don't have any money. . . . And [we have] debts over our eyebrows. But we've opened ten houses, and we spent the last two years developing our staff."

Covenant House became "legitimate." Unfortunately, however, Father Ritter says Covenant House has to "turn away ten, fifteen, twenty kids a day. And we're the only agency in New York, as far as I know, that really practices open intake twenty-four hours a day, every day of the year. We don't screen kids out. We never close. Our rule is the empty bed. The next kid who calls or comes in gets it. A lot of people would like to do that; I think we're the only ones who really do it.

"Last year, 2600 kids tried to get into Covenant House. We had room for 508. We had to turn away over 2,000 kids. This year we expect over 4,000 kids to try. . . . We'll have room for 600. No more than that. Most of them will be black and Spanish, eighty per cent. Eighty-five per cent will be from New York City. Most will be between fourteen and sixteen. Two thousand last year were between fourteen and sixteen . . . My experience is that most kids [who] are runaways don't have a place to really go back to.

From Huckleberry Finn to Huckleberry House

Almost always when I call the parents of a runaway child, almost always the answer I get back is, 'We don't want them; you keep them. If you send him home, we'll have him arrested.'

"So I'll turn to the kid and say something like, well, your mother said it's okay for you to live with us. But he knows what it means, he knows. . . ."

Father Ritter handed me a sheet of what might be called "Ritter-grams"; letters, in mimeo form, that he sends to supporters. One sheet was about "Billy." It tells about the youngster and how Covenant House works.

"Billy is tall, skinny, vacant-eyed, totally alert. . . . He's sitting there, facing me across my desk. He was found yesterday by a priest, huddled in the doorway of one of the churches here in New York. Billy ran away from home six cold days ago and he's been sleeping in phone booths, public lavatories and subways ever since. He's 13. . . .

" 'I'll call home,' he said. . . . 'Ma. I ain't coming home. I just ain't. . . . You said that last time. I ain't coming home. I ain't coming home . . . that's not it, sure I love you . . . I ain't coming home . . . Never mind . . . I can't tell you . . . I'm not in Ohio. I'm not anywhere I'm going to tell you. I have rights . . . I know I'm only 13. I ain't coming home, Mom. I ain't coming home. I can't tell you. It's no use asking questions. I'm okay, Mom. I'll keep in touch. I ain't coming home, Mommy. Goodbye. I'll call you to-morrow. Goodbye, Mommy, I can't come home. It's no use. I ain't coming home.' He was crying pretty hard by then.

" 'My father is old and sick and he's drunk a lot. He beats

123

me all the time. He's invented some pretty weird punishments for me. You wouldn't believe what he does to me.' He told me. It was pretty sick.

"We always believe a kid. We have to. We can't take the chance, for the kid's sake. There are too many thousands of cases of child abuse to take that chance. Most of the time it's not really true. Maybe a mother or father got mad and punished a child—but maybe they had good reason and the kid exaggerated—but we won't take the chance, for the kid's sake," Father Ritter wrote.

Three thousand miles away a similar scene was taking place in another facility.

"That's similar to how we got started . . .," Brian Slattery of Youth Advocates, Inc. (which runs Huckleberry House) told me in San Francisco.

"There was a covert message that the only way you get services, whether they be transportation, the hopes of a foster placement, an investigation of an allegation of abuse . . . the only way that would be allowed at Huckleberry's was if we turned the kids in to the juvenile justice system. We've always seen that as their choice. And we'll gladly help them do it. But that's *not* what they're coming for and not what we're all about," Mr. Slattery stated.

He was one of the witnesses who had testified before Senator Bayh's 1972 hearings on the Runaway Youth Act. I asked him if he still saw the issue of runaways the same way now as then.

"Yeah. I recently reread the testimony. I still see runaways the same way. The figures would differ, the percentages vary some. The most important thing . . . the work remains the same as it was."

Huckleberry House's origins can be traced back to 1967. That was also the year when the "only significant federally sponsored research in the area of runaway youth" was published, Brian Slattery said. The study, conducted by Dr. Robert Shellow and colleagues, showed that "the problems facing most runaway adolescents are the same as those facing many other young people. In this sense, running away from home can be seen as one way of dealing with these problems. Other adolescents deal with these problems differently, but not necessarily in ways that are better either for themselves or for the community."

"The specific recommendation [of the study]," Mr. Slattery told Senator Bayh's committee, "was to take recognition of the fact that the runaway crisis offers a unique opportunity to give assistance to families when they most want it, and to wait at all may be to wait too long. Their recommendation was that communities set up around-the-clock, on-the-spot, emergency aid services for teenagers and their families.

"In 1967, Huckleberry House became the first such center."

Huckleberry's has seen thousands of young people pass through its doors. According to Geoffrey Link, they get "fifty new kids a month through Huck's," though "not all stay." There are also "100 kids a month on long-term counseling. . . ."

"As a system, we're definitely seeing more kids," the youthful Link said. (Most of these workers seem to be in their twenties and thirties.)

The "system" includes group homes, food, counseling,

legal aid, alternative places to live, family therapy, drug care, medical help, and jobs. Like other nonprofit centers, Huck's also needs funds for its staff and the services it provides, one of which is its own hotline.

Their 1973 annual report notes that "Twenty per cent more clients are receiving significantly more services than a year ago. The staff is three times its former size. And annual expenditures are 10 times the original yearly budget." (Their 1974 budget was something like $400,000.)

One client who made use of the Huckleberry House system was Rick Wagner. We met Rick earlier, when he testified before the Bayh committee. Now we'll meet him again, some three years later.

Rick was fourteen when he testified. "At that time, I was living across the street [at Huckleberry House] waiting for placement into another foster home," Rick told me. "Right now, me and my brother just have our own place," he added. Rick, by the way, is also on the staff of Youth Advocates. He does some basic bookkeeping.

As Rick looks back, "it seems almost like a fantasy. But I was able to survive with the help of friends, and living by this guy for two weeks . . . without either of his parents knowing. How he did that, I don't know. Through the help of friends, I would get food and a place to stay. . . . When I first went to Huck's [it] was not too long after I found out about Huck's," he stated.

After talking with Rick for a bit, I headed back to Huck's which is across the street from Youth Advocates. There I was able to listen in on a counseling session with Gerty, a volunteer; Subiami, a counselor; and Frank, a client. (You might remember reading about Frank earlier in the book. The girl he was traveling with was raped, and she was unable to go to the police because she was a runaway.)

The session went something like this:

SUBIAMI: Tell me what happened. (The volunteer does the initial interview. Then the counselor sits in and tries to map out a strategy.)

FRANK: I was staying at these friends of mine, and one of them got arrested. She's in jail now. And the other moved out and left me in the apartment. Her friends were going in and out, you know, after she left. And my tickets were lying next to me and I was asleep. When I woke, they were gone. It really sort of messed up my head for a second. I really sort of got confused. Where shall I turn? you know . . . I ran away from Montana. I'm trying to get back now. I just wanted to leave, to sort of find myself. I wanted to get a job for the summer and go back to school. I have a job promised.

SUBIAMI: Now here's one game plan. You can turn yourself in to juvenile hall . . . fill out what we call a face sheet — which gives them information . . . like where you come from, etc. Under the law, they'll contact your folks and see if they can muscle the money out of your parents. [Subiami was not immediately aware that Frank was an orphan.] If your parents stick to their story—they don't have funds—the state of Montana will provide the transportation. I see that as being your only situation . . . unless you can find a . . . job. [He warns Frank that San Francisco has a high unemployment rate.] You could be housed here . . . nonstatus offenders here are not required to stay within the confines of juvenile hall. . . .

(Frank is an only child and a recent orphan. He was living with his grandmother, of whom he was very fond. He said he kept in touch with her by mail and, of course, called her—a must—when he came to Huck's. Meanwhile, he was negotiating with some relatives to come up with the money to replace the bus tickets that had been stolen. Eventually, the family came up with the money which, I was told, was used to pay for the bus home under a "hardship fare" case.)

Then there was Michelle. Age: fifteen. A bundle of energy, Michelle ran away for the first time when she was fourteen. "It was like my mother would never let me go out. Never. Out—anywhere out. You know, I would have to be home 3:10 when school was out at 3. And it was a fifteen-minute walk!"

She said her parents, who are divorced, split when she was seven.

"I couldn't do anything, you know. She would just embarrass me so much. I could never sleep over at other girls' houses."

The first time she ran away was with a friend, and they were gone a few days. Michelle came back, only to leave again ten days later.

"It got to the point," she said, "where it wasn't really running away. It was just to go out. I mean just for a little while."

Her mother's reaction, she said, was a tearful one. She said her mother had been in a mental hospital and was home on "heavy tranquilizers."

" 'Why did you do this to me?' she'd say," Michelle said about her mother. "She'd say, 'I'm a good mother,' and all that jive."

Her mother also called the police "a couple of times, but like they came over and got a description of me, but I never got caught. Because I didn't do anything stupid like ripping people off or stealing cars and stuff. That's when you get busted, man."

In the meantime, she said, police would have to be looking for a girl with her description and, "There's a billion girls with my height, and weight, and looks."

Michelle also said she got tired of sleeping on the beach and "having to practically go to bed with everybody everytime I wanted a place to sleep, you know. I just wanted a place for some sleep and food. It's cold outside. I wasn't scared exactly. I was just scared of not having a place to sleep. I was also scared of being caught. More than anything, I was scared of going home."

Michelle came to Huck's and Youth Advocates by way of her guidance counselor. When I met her, she was waiting to be placed in a foster home under voluntary placement.

There are scores of runaway centers around the country.

They cater to a maximum of about 100,000 youths a year, the Office of Youth Development's Ed Farley said. Or about 10 per cent of the reported runaways annually.

Perhaps it was Lorraine who best summed up the need for such centers. The sixteen-year-old, five-time runaway (the first time was at age eleven) stated that she thought, "if you're serious about getting away from home, you should come to a place like this [Huck's] and not keep running. Cause you're safe here, you know, and you can get what you want in terms of a group home or foster home. It's not safe on the street. . . . Well, you know, anything could happen to you. You could even be murdered tomorrow, for all you know. . . .

7.

Runaway House

The first time I visited Runaway House in Washington, D.C., was 1972. Now it was the summer of 1975, and I was seated in the basement of Runaway House, which serves as the headquarters for Special Approaches to Juvenile Assistance (SAJA, Inc.), which is, in effect, the counterpart to Youth Advocates in San Francisco.

As the heat and humidity turned the Washington streets into a flat waffle-iron, three of us sat in the air-conditioned confines of the basement. The three were: Marjorie Statman of SAJA, Onnie Charlton of Runaway House, and myself.

I began by asking Ms. Statman her thoughts about any changes that may have occurred during the past several years.

"My initial impression," she said, "was that Runaway House was a renegade institution with renegade counselors and renegade kids. And that most of the kids were going somewhere and wouldn't stop for any help. And I'm not sure that they were different kids than we're seeing today.

I think that the orientation towards seeking help has changed. Rather than who the kids are that are coming.

"These were the same kids who were at Haight-Ashbury as we see today. They're more receptive to help. There are fewer alternatives. I mean there's been a kind of disillusionment around what one can go out and do on their own. The generation of the flower children has died. And the kids are much more cynical about being able to go out and create new life styles and new lives for themselves. There was a time of economic plenty in this country and that has definitely changed. It's difficult for a kid to make it on his own," Ms. Statman explained.

Ms. Charlton commented that "a runaway could have pretty much crashed with anyone when it was the thing to do, and now they can't do that. But the trust for people had to diminish because of what was happening in the world. And now they have to have a Runaway House, whereas before the necessity wasn't as great."

But the change has not only been on the side of the juveniles. It has affected the workers as well. As Ms. Statman noted, "We're much more oriented to working with them [the establishment, police, and courts] than we had been in the past. One of the things I think we've learned over the years was that those people themselves are not our enemies—that the institutions that they work in are. The people within those institutions have the ability to be flexible, and, if you work toward them, get them to understand where you're coming from—rather than have a hostile attitude toward them from the beginning—you can get a lot of stuff done. And that's changed enormously."

We also discussed the types of youths—the clients— Runaway House gets now, as compared with a few years ago. They too have changed. By comparison with the "average" fourteen-year-old white girl from the suburbs, for example, "there's another kind of average runaway who's a black ghetto kid who's sixteen, and been through three relatives already," says Ms. Statman.

"That's a trend that we've seen changed," Ms. Charlton explained, "especially in the last year. . . . Runaway houses served mostly white kids from the suburbs. The number of blacks we have served from the ghettos as opposed to middle class blacks has increased in the last year."

"I know that 20 per cent of the kids we've seen over the last year have been black ghetto kids. It was . . . a negligible amount before that," Ms. Statman said. She added, "There's another average kid, white or black, who has run from an institution, and who has been institutionalized almost all their lives, whether in foster homes or in an actual institutional setting. . . .

"Legally, we are required to return kids to institutions. But the way we deal with that is by dealing with their probation officers and caseworkers. Most of the kids that come to us from institutions are kids that . . . have been status offenders. And the caseworkers are very happy to let us find another alternative. They don't want them back in the institutions. They have no options themselves. And when we're willing to do the casework involved in finding another alternative, they're very happy to let them stay at Runaway House, and for us to do most of that work.

"And there's a clear distinction," Ms. Statman continued,

"between the kids—middle class and lower class—in terms of what happens to them when they run away. Psychiatric Institute in Washington is filled with adolescents who have run away from home. And those are adolescents who come from Montgomery County [Md.], and Virginia counties. And they're all white, middle-class kids. The same kids doing the very same things from the lower-class black families in the District of Columbia end up in one of the correctional institutions.

"Runaway House," Ms. Statman also notes, "is still a crisis center." But, "counseling is the important thing." She went on. "Kids can stay at RH as long as they are working on their situation. Sometimes we reach dead ends with kids where there's nothing they want to work on and there's nothing that they want to do and they have to leave without there being any real solution. But we've had kids stay for months when they've been in family counseling, and the goal all along was that they would be going home. We've had other kids staying for months waiting for a placement, because they couldn't go home."

Some youths also get referred to RH through the courts when there is no other place to send them except the local juvenile hall. Most stay for a day or two, the youth workers explained, while the court is deciding what to do with them. But some, like youths from out of town, may stay as long as two weeks, while waiting for their parents to be contacted.

"Our whole philosophy in working with kids," Marjorie Statman stated, "is towards getting them to take the steps that have to be taken. . . . They've run away; and that's an act of some kind of independence—it's a positive act—and they have to follow through on whatever has to happen as a result of that act."

Ms. Statman added that minors "have to deal with their parents or whoever they're in the custody of, in order for any alternative to happen. . . . They need their parents' permission to live in an alternative kind of placement. They need their parents to be in family counseling if that's what they want. They need permission from a social worker, if they're in the court custody, to go live in a group home. And so, most alternatives that kids come up with, their parents have to be involved in some way. And that's what we counsel towards."

The age of majority in Washington, D.C., is eighteen. Three-quarters of the clients RH sees are girls averaging around fifteen or sixteen. The boys are about the same age, too. The majority of these juveniles come from broken homes, although the majority of those in counseling are from intact families, the SAJA people explained.

"Most of our kids go home," Ms. Statman indicated. "A vast majority of them end up going home." But many come back again. "We have a very high [repeat] rate. And I don't see that as being negative. . . . I think there are two things involved in that."

First, she said, "is that a kid who's in a really bad situation at home has to run away four or five times before anybody is going to recognize that anything bad is going on. And that if you bring a kid into court after the first run away, they'll send him home. If you bring a kid into the court after the sixth time they've run away, somebody might take notice. Or the parents might get disgusted enough to bring them into court. And some kind of actions start happening.

"The other thing is," she added, "that we have a whole lot of kids who go home pretty much . . . intent on living at home . . . [and] don't want to live anyplace else. But every once in a while something explodes and they need to get away for a while. And they come to Runaway House and they have a breather of a couple of days. Most of them call their parents, tell them they're at Runaway House, and go home after a few days. And they just need time and space away from their families. . . ."

We also discussed the services available to youths at Runaway House, which seem to be pretty similar to Huckleberry House's, in terms of referral, counseling, and long-term care.

"We have two long-term group homes, a temporary group home, which is up to six months, and we have a foster care program," Ms. Statman explained.

"And I think they're all pretty unique. The foster care program is unique in that it does not see itself as placing kids in other families. It by and large doesn't choose nuclear families as a place to place kids. We've licensed communes, we've licensed single individuals, young college students. And mostly what the placement is geared towards is finding an older friend for the kids to live with, rather than a new family. And what happens out of that is that the patterns that have developed in the person's original family don't have to replay themselves in this new family.

"And the other thing," Ms. Statman went on, "is that kids can have more contact with their own families, because the families don't see the foster placement as competition for them. They don't see the people who are taking care of their kids as the new parents. So that's the foster program.

"The group homes are unusual in that they're run pretty democratically. The kids, within limits, make the rules in the house. They pretty much live communally. Again, the counselors who live there are not parents. . . . So it doesn't try to mimic a nuclear family. (At times, however, youths do want another family, and on those occasions, an effort will be made to place them there.)

"The other thing that's unique is that we do weekly supervisions—that foster placement gets essentially family counseling weekly. And, in most traditional agencies, once a kid gets placed in a home, the social worker will only visit once a month, if that often," said Ms. Statman, who holds a graduate degree in social work.

I was also told that, unlike more traditional agencies, Runaway House aims at "what the kid wants," as opposed to the more discretionary "what-is-best-for-the-kid" approach.

Runaway House also has at its disposal free clinics, a public defenders' service, a local university's juvenile justice clinic, and local community health centers, including private psychiatrists and psychologists. The staff also makes use of "Travelers Aid for transportation, to get a kid home or back to their own state."

Like other such centers, RH gets public and private funds.

The reasons youths come in, Ms. Statman said, include, " 'My father won't let me date,' 'I have to be home before it's dark,' 'my parents found dope in my room.' . . . These reasons are in addition to cases of abuse and cases of alcoholism. But, as Ms. Charlton pointed out, "It's generally [because] there's emotional stuff happening in the family where the member's needs are not being met through the family system. Very often the kids that we receive become the scapegoat of the family. And are receiving the brunt of most people's anger. And that's basically it."

Ms. Statman also mentioned that such problems as "the long-hair thing," which apparently no longer creates the friction it used to, is, nevertheless, to her, seen "as symptoms and not as problems."

Sometimes, however, the family and the youths must be separated. But, said Ms. Charlton, "The first option we explore is the return of the kid to home." Because "to separate a family is a very heavy decision to make. And the situation has to be so heavy for the kid to go home that it's an impossibility. It also has to be pretty much [a situation where] both parents and the kid agree, that the kid shouldn't be home. But it's much better for everyone involved, if the kid can go home—if the family can get family counseling—and things can be straightened out."

"We try," Ms. Statman told me, "to work with the family and the kid, and together come to some kind of decision about what should be done."

Accordingly, there are a number of options available for the juvenile. They range from getting the young person back home to placing him or her with a friend or relative, or obtaining some alternative kind of setting like a foster home.

"Foster placement," Ms. Statman said, "doesn't have to involve the court. You see, it's only $125 a month that the foster parent or family receives. So the kid can work and earn part of that money. The parents can pay a lot of times. And, if the parents are willing to sign permission for the kid to live in that home, then there's no need for any kind of court action."

Group homes, on the other hand, are more expensive. They cost a minimum of $500 a month. And the costs are increasing along with other costs for maintaining each youth. So, says the SAJA director, "it's unrealistic to think that a family could pay for that. Or that a kid could earn that. So . . . then our only option is to go through court and get money through the courts."

Unfortunately, Ms. Statman says, "the thing about the court process is that there is no way to go to court and there [have] a mutual decision that the kid shouldn't be living at home. The way the courts are set up, either the kid is to blame or the parents are to blame. So, either the parents have to file [a] PINS petition saying the kid is out of control. Or you have to prove neglect. And to prove neglect, then the parents are guilty. And to prove out of control, then the kid is guilty. So there is no way to go in and say this family shouldn't be together. I've never heard of it being different anyplace. . . ."

Furthermore, court jurisdiction may be called for if the parents want the child, but the youth doesn't want the parents. Or, again, if the parents can't afford to have the child stay in one of those homes.

Lesley is a client of Runaway House. She is fourteen.

The first time she ran away she was twelve. She had been

afraid to run before by herself. Finally, she took off with a friend.

Lesley ran away, she said, "because my mom was having all these kinds of financial problems. And I mean she would go into a depression. You know, she couldn't afford all this stuff, and so she felt bad and would go into a depression. And I was tired of that. Otherwise, she was all right. But the depression was like every day. It was horrible."

Her parents, she said rather wistfully, were divorced. "I don't even remember my father. I faintly, like barely, remember him. We haven't had a father since then."

Lesley also said she resented the fact that her mother wouldn't let her out at night. When Lesley ran away, she was also getting back at her mother. For example, when she came to Runaway House, Lesley and a counselor called her mother.

"She was worried out of her brain," Lesley explains. "I was having fun though. She said, 'Where are you? Are you freezing? Are you standing in a phone booth? Are you okay?' And I go, 'Yeah, I'm hanging in there.' I didn't want to make it sound like I was doing all right, because I was mad.

"Yeah, I was mad at her. Torturing me. Not letting me go outside. It was horrible. No, it would be come home from school, do your homework, run outside for tennis, and run back in the house. And strand us in the house all night. I'd say, '*Please* let me go outside.' And she'd say, 'No.'"

Lesley also got herself busted. For shoplifting, she said. Right now she was on probation. "It taught me a lesson.

I don't want to get busted again. Because if I do, I'll have to go to a detention center in Virginia, because I've already been caught once, and I have a record," she explained.

When I left Lesley, she was at one of SAJA's group homes, waiting to be placed in a foster home.

One runaway—actually an ex-runaway—that I ran into in Washington was Mouse Norris. He, along with Becky Lovelace, had testified at the Bayh hearings in 1972. I sought him out to see what progress he was making.

Apparently, Mouse is doing okay. And, for that matter, he said, so is Becky.

"I'm in school," he told me. "And Becky's working."

Mouse, now twenty-one, is also on the board of trustees of SAJA, and he's gotten involved in the issue of runaways "from the other end."

"I never went back home," he added.

8.

Teaneck Home

Dinnertime. The sights and sounds of eight pretty, lively girls and the smell of meatballs, lasagna, salad, bread, and iced tea. Laughter and giggling. Yelling and the clanking of dishes. A dozen people gathered around a dinner table. Not an unusual scene.

This was different from the ordinary home meal, for this was no ordinary home. This was the Teaneck Home for Girls in Teaneck, New Jersey. Although it is run with the support of the National Council of Jewish Women, the Teaneck Home takes in girls of all religions.

I had been invited for dinner. I was, in a sense, the guest of honor. The girls were very careful to see that I was made comfortable. Did I have enough tea? Did I want more bread? Would I like salad dressing? Did I mind if they smoked? Smoking is one "vice" such homes permit. As with other places, sex, drugs, and alcohol are prohibited under penalty of banishment—getting kicked out.

I was seated at the head of the table. At the other end

sat Mary Jane Keidel and her husband, Ernst—the house-parents—and their daughter, Heidi, age two. Along the sides of the table sat eight teenagers: Vickie, seventeen (whom we met before); Liza, seventeen; Rhea, nineteen; Lana, seventeen; Denise, seventeen; Toni, fourteen; Jodi, thirteen; and Bonnie, seventeen. (Bonnie went home that night, so we never got a chance to talk.)

If the dinner scene appeared routine for a large family (which is what they are to a great extent), the table conversation belied that. For these were girls who had run away or were taken away from their parents.

Seventeen-year-old Lana explained. "I was in a detention center for thirty-one days. And for only one reason. A bad foster home. Really bad. I got taken away from my parents last year, because of child abuse. My father tried to kill me.

"So I was sent to this foster home. And the husband made advances toward me. When the wife found out, she started slipping me some pills. One day I started throwing up, you know. And I fainted. And I banged my head. And my eye started bleeding. So she brought me to the hospital. And I told them what happened. The woman's husband left her. And they didn't know where to put me. There were no other foster homes available. So I was there thirty-one days."

Eventually, Lana was sent to another foster home. This one didn't work out either. Lana said she felt like she was an "intruder." So she "tripped out" on pills and got sent to the hospital, having to drop out of school as a result.

"And then I went to another foster home, and, finally,

143

I said I wanted to go home. So I went home and got taken away again, five months ago. And now I'm here."

Her experiences have taught her one thing, Lana said. "I'm not going to have nothing to do with the state. I'm just going to get out on my own, you know, when I'm eighteen. The state's messed me up in too many ways. Like, I appreciate everything they tried to do for me. And I understand that it's not their fault that I was put in foster homes. But I've had too much experience with them. I want to be on my own. I feel like my whole life, since I've gone through the state, has been run by clocks and people. And I feel kind of like a machine, you know. Like I had to come in at a certain time, and do all these things. Like if I really don't want to come home to dinner, it's so much of a hassle, you know. And I can't do it. I just want to be able to do what I want, when I want."

I asked Lana if she could describe what her thirty-one days in detention were like.

"I was only on the ninth floor for one day. And that's, you know, where the crazy people go. And then, when you get better, they send you down to the eighth floor. I was there for only one night. Like, I was surrounded by all these really messed-up people, you know? And none of them knew where their heads was at. I really didn't know where my head was at, but, you know, I wasn't there for a reason, you know what I mean. I wasn't there for being crazy.

"What I did the whole time I was there," Lana continued, "I kind of talked to a lot of people . . . I turned myself, I guess, into kind of a 'shrink'. . . . And, at first, I didn't mind being there. But then it got to be ten days, and then eleven days. And it got to the point where I threatened to call the newspapers . . . because it was illegal what they were doing to me. Because I wasn't taking any medication. The only medication I was taking was sleeping pills, because I fell out of bed one night when I was having a nightmare. But it was up to me whether I wanted to take them or not. Like I wasn't seeing a psychiatrist while I was there. Maybe once a week. You know, he was waiting for this place to open.

"And I just flipped out . . . because like they weren't doing anything to get me out of there, you know what I mean. Like they were, but they weren't trying hard enough. . . . They just left me there. They just forgot about me."

"I'll tell you why I'm here," Denise joined in. "Me and my mother had an argument, and I said I can't take it no more. You know, I OD'd once. And I said I can't take this no more. My mother called the police and filed a complaint on me. They put me in the same place where Lana was. I'll tell you what it's like. It's some place where you don't want to be.

"It's got a backyard with a fence around it and everything. So I got a lawyer from this woman (who got her here in the first place). She was going to court on Monday, so I spent the weekend there.

"You see, my parents, especially my mother, are from the old country, and they're strict. She wanted to bring me up the way she was brought up, and I couldn't take that. Like my mother, I went home to visit her the other day . . . like I still have feelings for her. And I brought her some spearmint she makes tea with. And I had a teeny hickey on my neck. A little one. And right away, she calls me a prostitute. She was going to send me to the doctor. That's how she talks. 'Look at that,' she says to my father. 'You're killing me,' she says.

"My father, he listens to my mother. He yesses her. And I can't take that. They're divorced, you know. Because he's an alcoholic, and because he needs her, however, they still live together.

"I don't think my father's an alcoholic," Denise said, "but she's convinced him to the point that he cannot live without her. She's got him brainwashed.

"So he went back to her," Denise continued, "and now she has him on a leash. . . ."

Beyond that, Denise said, her mother did things to her that made life unbearable at home. "She says all my friends are bums. And she wants me to stay in and be like she was. I stayed home and I cooked the dinner. I stayed home and cleaned the house. . . . You know, she used to punish me. She slapped me across the mouth when I was little. She used to take away my clothes and make me wear the same things every day. She wouldn't let me take a shower—that was punishment. That's why I'm a shower freak now. She'd break my records. She'd call up my friends' houses. I don't need that, you know. So I just left.

"You know, I would sit down with my mother and I would tell her things, you know. And then regret I told her. Because she would use it against me."

One day, out of anger, Denise said she tore the phone off the wall. Her mother called the police.

"She called the police and said I beat her and everything. The police were on their way, and I was going to run. But then I said, why should I run away? They're gonna pick me up and really think I did it. So I sat there and waited for the cops. And they took me down to the police station. I thought they were going to take me to the detention center. And I thought, that's not fair. It's not fair. So I got a lawyer and I won at court. And that's why I'm here."

At one point, Denise said, she OD'd on pills. She ended up in a mental institution. She was sent there by the court, she said. She ran away from there, was brought back, and eventually sent to the Teaneck home. I asked her to describe the mental institution.

"You're just a thing there, you know. Like over here, people have emotions. People care about themselves. Over there, they had so many kids there, they don't really understand. They know you by papers. They know you by what people said, by psychiatrists. But they don't know you. Like I know you [points to Lana] from school. But now I know you better. Because when you live with a person, you know what they're like. But there, if they read a paper, right away, they think they know your whole life. . . .

"And you couldn't wear your own clothes at lunch hour. And they told you when you could take a shower. And no snacking. You can't eat when you want. You can be starving. They feed you crud. That's what they feed you. I ate potatoes every day in that place. You get fed crud and they expect you to hold that crud in your stomach all night without anything else.

"That's why," Denise continued, "I say, to me, this is like

147

a home. I consider it my home. Because I figure, I'm going to live here till I'm eighteen. And it's my home. So I don't say I'm in a group home. I say this is my house."

Nonetheless, Denise says she misses her natural home. "I still have feelings for my mother," she told me. "Sure at times I hate her. But, you know, when you're away . . . I miss home. Even though you've always been away from it, home will always be home. . . . And, what can I do? He's my father, but . . . I could be without him, you know? I'll be old enough to be on my own."

"My parents' relationship was called sado-masochism," Lana began again. "Well, my father beat the heck out of my mother. Literally. Like, he kicked my mother in the nose, and he split her nose. You could see the skin, right there. It was horrible. Like he was very violent. He threw my brother down on concrete and chipped his teeth. And like he strangled me. And my relationship with my brother was that he was my sanity. And I was his sanity.

"Like when my father is beating my mother," Lana continued, "he like gets to the point where he can't stop, and he's actually enjoying it. And like my mother hates to get hit. But, afterwards, like walking around with black eyes and everything, she loves it. Because then my father feels so bad . . . if you can understand it. It's weird."

Suddenly Lana bolted from the table and shot out of the room. Apparently one of the younger girls had giggled. Lana was crushed.

"She's a very unhappy person, you shouldn't make fun of her," Mary Jane reprimanded Toni, the offender.

"I didn't," Toni replied.

"You're sitting there guffawing," retorted Mary Jane.

"She was coming out with some good points," Denise added.

There was a brief discussion about Lana's outburst, and then we began to talk to some of the other girls. Up to that time, the two most outspoken girls were Lana and Denise. Now some of the other girls had a chance to tell their stories.

"I didn't run away," Rhea, nineteen, told me. "I was kicked out. My mother used to say, 'I'll never throw my children out.' When I told her this, she said to me: 'Are you my child?'

"My parents kicked me out four times," Rhea continued. "Because I was going to school and worked on two jobs, and my mother expected me to do all the work—to do her work. Clean the clothes, take care of the kids, cook dinner, and I would. I cooked dinner for my father and stuff, and it just got monotonous, and I couldn't do it. And she just called me names and kicked me." Rhea also said that she was headed for home at the end of the summer. Her mother was no longer there, and her father wanted her home.

Then there's thirteen-year-old Jodi.

"I got here through a social worker," Jodi explained. "I've been sent away since I'm nine years old. And now I'm thirteen. I was sent away because my mother and I, we just don't get along.

"Like when I first came here, I went home one weekend, and I wanted to go out and stay by my girlfriend's house for the night. And my mother got really mad at me. She didn't want me to. But my father is nice to me sometimes because he's my stepfather.

"One time, too," Jodi told me, "my mother asked me to come home to discuss things." So Jodi went home. Again, she wanted to stay with a friend. But this time, she said, her mother beat her. Now, she says, her mother is nice to her "because she wants me to forget about it. But I just can't forget about it. Like that was the first time she had ever really done anything that really bad or anything."

Jodi's long hair also seems to be a bone of contention between mother and daughter.

"When I was ten, I had hair down to my behind, and my mother didn't like it, because I didn't know how to take care of it. But she would always take care of it. But she got sick and tired of doing it. So she just cut it. She took me to a beauty parlor and she just got it cut. And from then on, whenever I have long hair, she always cuts it on me. She wants to cut it now. And I don't want her to."

Jodi also confided to me that she had first been sent to "two boarding schools, and they took me out of there, because I was doing too many bad things up there. I was a monster. I don't want to go into it. And my mother took me out for those reasons, and like, everybody knows about them. . . ."

Now, Jodi told me proudly, "I get merit certificates. I've gotten so many since I've been here. I got one for a baby-sitting course. And I got one that President Nixon signed [for physical fitness]."

The hour was getting late. It had been a long evening.

With the girls generally preoccupied with their own activities, and with Ernst gone off to work, Mary Jane and I had an opportunity to talk.

We sat in the coolness of the only room that is really hers and Ernst's, the master bedroom. And even that is subject to intrusion. Nevertheless, with Heidi safely resting—if somewhat restlessly—in the lap of her mother, Mary Jane and I began to talk.

My first question was whether or not what the girls were telling me was, in fact, the truth. I had already been warned by others—police and youth workers—that the youngsters sometimes had a tendency to exaggerate. Sometimes exaggerating to the point where they actually believe their own stories.

Was what the girls told me generally the truth?

"It's true, yes," Mary Jane told me. "We have runaways, mainly. We have Toni—you didn't talk to her much—but she has no one. No one at all. And she hasn't been in any trouble in any way. They just didn't know where to place her."

She continued, "Jodi's the little one. She's been taken away from her mother because of child abuse. We also have kids who've been in a little bit of trouble. Nothing major. Like they were caught smoking pot or drinking. And they didn't know where to put them.

"Most of the kids we have, their parents are separated. And they can't live with one parent, or they're thrown back and forth. So that's mainly what we've had so far. But mostly, we've had kids who just couldn't make it at home, for one reason or another."

151

"How do the kids get here?" I asked.

When a kid's in trouble, Mary Jane told me, she calls the local helpline. That's one way. Or sometimes the school will call. "Sometimes the police bring them over. They find them on the street. . . . We've even had a couple of girls just walk right through the door, like Rhea." Or they hear about the Teaneck Home through word of mouth, from friends.

"What I do is notify the police, because the parents will be looking for her, and I can't just take a girl off the street and keep her here. And the police will usually notify the parents. And we have a permission slip they [the parents] have to sign giving us the authority. Some parents don't want to sign it. Then it has to go through the courts, where they may take the kid away from the parents. Sometimes the kid can't stay here. The parents refuse to sign any papers, and they want the kid home.

"And then a few days go by and everything cools off and the kid goes back home. And then you find another few days, the kid comes back again.

"Denise was our first. And they have sort of a soft spot inside for her. And she's gotten into quite a lot of trouble, but they keep taking her back. In some ways she may be mature, but in other ways, no.

"Just recently, she tried to kill herself. She was sleeping upstairs, and I went upstairs to see why she hadn't come down for dinner. She said, 'I'm just tired.' And I looked in her eyes, and she looked bad."

The Keidels took Denise to the hospital. "She was in a coma for three days," Mary Jane recalled. "And this time, after that, she was a changed person. She's a little dizzy [they call her 'scatterbrain']. I think what she did to herself had something to do with it.

"In fact, I just got word today that Denise will be moved on by the end of this month. She doesn't even know. I don't know where.

"There's no real place for Denise," Mary Jane explained. "Because she's in the middle. She needs more structure than a group home can give her. But to put her in a place like [a detention center] is too rough for her. The kids are too rough for her [there]. She needs something in the middle. And there is no such place. So she's going to go home, which is not the answer."

I mentioned to Mary Jane that Denise told me that you can't be negative on yourself, because other people will be. And that she wouldn't try to kill herself because she does love herself.

"She developed that philosophy," Mary Jane said, "and she tells people that. And she tries very hard to believe in it herself. She developed that philosophy before she tried to kill herself. And she was trying to help another girl who was very depressed for a time, and she got depressed herself.

"And she tried very hard to live by that. But sometimes things become too much for her. I find that when she has trouble at home. Or a boyfriend doesn't work out. Or she has a fight with a girlfriend—the whole world is . . . beat. Because she doesn't do very well in school . . . and that's her whole life—her friends."

I told Mary Jane that Denise told me that she couldn't

stand it at home. Yet here they were going to send her back.

"Well, when the girls come here, they're told the rules. And Denise's been here a few times and asked to leave here a few times. And they always took her back. And she knows what the rules are. She's trying hard to live by the rules, but she hasn't been able to. And I guess they're at the point now where they feel they've given her many chances and she's . . . blown them.

"They found a pot plant she was growing in her room. And that's one of the main rules: no drugs!"

Mary Jane said that Lana was scheduled to be sent home, too. "She hasn't gone to school all year."

"Most of the kids here have such a bad family life," she added. "None ever had any birthdays or holidays where they sat together at dinner.

"Lana's family," she noted, "was the worst in DYFS [Division of Youth and Family Services] history. She'll get into trouble and then her parents will sign a complaint against her and she'll end up in [juvenile hall] or a [mental] institution. . . . There should be some middle kind of thing between a group home and an institution. Sometimes foster [care] is considered middle."

Mary Jane explained that "each girl has her own caseworker." They also receive support from the National Council of Jewish Women and the Division of Youth and Family Services.

"Most of the girls who live here are sixteen and seventeen. A girl can stay till she's eighteen." Toni could stay until she was eighteen because "she has no parents."

"She had a father and a stepmother," Mary Jane explained. "And the stepmother decided she didn't want to live there anymore with the husband. So she just ran away. And the husband, after a few months, took off after her. But the things he did before he left made it so they couldn't go back."

Before he left, the natural father took each of the girls to bed with him.

"And he has never been in touch," Mary Jane added. "They don't even know where he is.

"The next door neighbors took over the three girls who were there. And they were watching for a while, and the parents never came back. So they called the authorities." The neighbors then asked, and received, permission to be foster parents to the girls. But they in turn "proceeded to mess up the kids worse than they were messed up before." Each girl ran away, and then each girl ended up being separated from the others.

By now it was time for little Heidi to go to bed. After speaking with Mary Jane a bit longer, I had a chance to speak to Vickie. (We met her earlier; she had run away to join the carnival.)

Vickie was leaving for home that evening. Her boyfriend, Jack, had come to pick her up, along with her belongings —which included a huge stuffed teddy bear.

We spoke about the second time she ran away from home, and how she came to the Teaneck home. She ran, she said, because "I was having problems at home, and I happen to know one of the ladies that runs the place.

"The problem," she told me, "was between me and my little sister. My mother always stuck up for her. Whatever she did was right." The little sister, she said, was thirteen, and the product of her mother's second marriage.

"I wouldn't say it was running away," Vickie maintained. "Not at seventeen.

"Anyway, I told her I was leaving, and she said, 'Good!'

"When I first walked through the door [at the Teaneck Home], I couldn't believe it. I thought this was the most beautiful place. . . . I was expecting a prison, really, something like where the other girls stayed. But I drove up to a house on a normal street. It was a shock."

During her stay here, she said, her relations with her mother began to improve. After a couple of months, she was able to go home on weekends. "And I guess it just worked itself out. Well, it started a couple of months ago. Around my birthday. I was home weekends, and I noticed it wasn't that bad."

She also said she was getting along better with her stepsister.

She and her mother (whom we'll meet shortly) "talk now like we could never talk before. Before it was like she was the mother and I was the daughter. Now it's like on a friendly basis. I didn't have a relationship with my mother before. It was like she tells me what to do, and I listen. You know, I'm the daughter, she's the mother. Now it's like we're friends.

"It's strange how I could look back at it now and laugh sometimes. And I'm so different now. . . . Like nine months ago, we were at each other's throats. A lot has changed in

nine months. I think this place has done all the changing.
I think, for example, that I learned to cope with my little
sister by coming here. Because a lot of the girls are thirteen, fourteen, fifteen years old. We had a lot of problems
here, I mean. I mean there were nine girls here in the
home at one time, and there were a lot of arguments. But,
I don't know. It's funny. We were all pretty much of a
family here, because we all lived together as sisters. But I
learned to cope with the problems that the little ones had.
That the thirteen and fourteen-year-olds had," Vickie said.

"Rhea and I," she added, "are the oldest here. I'm
eighteen [she was going to be], and Rhea is nineteen. They
don't force you out when you're eighteen. It's just something that you're ready to do. Like my mother was ready
to take me and I was ready to go.

"I was ready to go long before, but I didn't want to, just
in case. I mean I didn't want anything to happen that could
mess up my graduation.

"Oh, yeah. Definitely. My mother went through changes.
A lot had to do with my stepfather. Because they were
having a lot of problems. She was nervous all the time.
Now he's gone, she's a lot calmer. She's changed. I can't
explain how she's changed.

"I remember one meeting I had with her. I told her that
one of the problems was that she was too cold. Because
she never opened up and let her feelings show towards her
children or towards me. And I'm very sensitive. I have
to know . . . that she cares or something. She was a hard
woman. She still is, but she's not so much anymore.

"I always knew she cared . . . well, I had a best friend

157

whose mother always, you know, gave her confidence. My mother never did that. You know, she wasn't the type of person to come out of nowhere and hug you. And say I love you. Now she does all the time. She's warmer now.

"I used to write her poetry," Vickie continued, "you know, I can say things better written. I can write how I feel. But it was hard for me to say how I feel. So I write her a lot of poetry. I think my graduation has a lot to do with it [their getting along better]. I think she was worried; holding back. I think she's proud. I'm older, too. But I think she learned also."

One thing that annoyed Vickie in particular had nothing to do with her mother. It was problems with the neighbors.

"Like one lady called us 'tenants in an institution.' I don't think that's what runaways are at all."

By now I was eager to speak with Vickie's mother. I wanted to find out how she saw things. I called her, and this is what she told me.

"Well, I was very upset that first time she [Vickie] ran away. Actually, to begin with, she wasn't running away. She was away on vacation, and she got the idea of going with a carnival while she was away. She was visiting her girl friend, and then, when she didn't come home, I didn't know what to do, you know. And I reported it to the police. And they were looking for her, but they had no luck finding her. And I just had to wait and hope that she would come back and that she would be all right.

"Yeah, she did call me after a while. I guess it was about two, three weeks. She called my other children and she spoke to them. But she didn't speak to me. She was afraid, I guess, that I would reprimand her.

"And then she got her fill of it and wanted to come home. She was in Maryland at the time, I think. And she went to one of those Traveler's Aids, and they called me. And I informed the police here. And they got in touch with the police in Maryland. And that's how we got her back."

She also confirmed that Vickie had been arrested because her school principal had reported her truant.

Did she and Vickie have any problems in communicating? I asked.

"Well, I didn't like her boyfriend. I still don't like him. And that was the cause of our problems this time. The first time around, it was that she wanted to see what there was to see. The carnival excited her. I mean, there was no reason, no argument or anything, that she ran away.

"She claims that she doesn't get along with her (little) sister, but I think that she was using that as an excuse. . . ."

"Did you feel," I asked, "that you had trouble communicating? And that you're communicating better now?"

"Oh, yeah. Well, we got along fine while she was living at the home. And she was home every weekend. It wasn't as though she were out of the house, and I wasn't letting her come into the house. She was here most of the time. She just slept there. And as long as Jack stayed away, everything was fine. No problem. It was only when he came around that we had problems."

What didn't she like about him? I wanted to know.

"He's crude," she told me. "He's arrogant; he's a kid. He's seventeen, but he's got the mind of a fifteen-year-old.

159

And he thinks the world owes him a living. And I just couldn't take it. And he walked all over his mother. And he thought he could do it with anybody. It's just the boy himself that I don't like.

"Yeah, he's still seeing her, and he comes around. But he's changed a bit. But I still don't have anything to do with him. As long as he behaves himself, I have no major objections.

"I had let him come into my house before. And he acted like he owned my house. You know, he'd go upstairs when he felt like it. Went into my refrigerator when he felt like it."

"Do you feel you had a problem communicating with Vickie before?" I asked.

"As far as he was concerned, yes," she answered. "But [with] anything else, there was no problem. We could sit and talk for hours, as long as his name wasn't mentioned. As soon as his name was mentioned, the air just . . . fogged. Now I stay away from the subject, and Vickie doesn't bring it up. I don't want to discuss him because we'd end up in an argument."

Finally, I asked Vickie's mother if she had any advice for parents, in terms of her own experience? Did she think that family counseling helped any?

"Well, you can't push, you know. I mean, I tried to stop her from seeing him. And that didn't work. I also tried reverse psychology. You know, like, I don't care. Just don't bring him near the house. Well, she's still seeing him. So it didn't do anything. I think when you're told, no, it makes you want it all the more. So I stopped. And I said,

I don't care. You want to see him, that's your business. But I don't want him near my house.

"As far as family counseling goes, I don't think it really helps," Vickie's mother said. "I mean, we've no problem in any other field except him. He was the big problem. And family counseling wasn't going to change my mind any. You know, if you're having problems in all areas, maybe family counseling would help. But he was the only problem, so I don't feel that family counseling would have helped."

She explained that she felt she and Vickie could avoid disrupting their lives together by avoiding Jack.

One last word about Denise and Lana. Some time after my visit, I called Mary Jane. I found out that Denise had been allowed to stay after all. Apparently, she had become so much a fixture there, the home could not send her away.

Unfortunately, the same could not be said about Lana. She ran away. The last I heard, she was headed for Colorado.

9.

On the Road: Getting Help

Dear Arnold:

Sorry I did not get a chance to speak with you when you were in San Francisco, but I did want to jot down some notes about the subject of runaways which you had asked me to comment about. . . .

The decision to run away by a pre-adolescent or adolescent is often a sign of considerable inner turmoil and interpersonal difficulties. Not infrequently, one finds that the child or young adult believes that they have no other recourse. They are unable to communicate their needs, their distress or aspirations to the parent figures or other significant adults in their environment. Hence, they run away. If the parents are divorced, they may run away from one parent to another . . . [But] if both parents are together, and the child runs away, you must consider the possibility that the child is fleeing from some current difficulty with one or both parental figures.

Some of the children that I have interviewed left home because they were suffering physical and/or emotional hostility which was intolerable. Other instances occur where the child is leaving a . . . situation where they are the victim of parental sexual assault. At times the individual youngster has spoken with teachers or physicians in the hopes that someone would offer a reasonable alternative. Failing that, they may choose to flee but often without direction. . . .

Ultimately, one cannot make a generalization which fits all kinds of runaways. It is not necessarily a sign of poor mental health. Indeed, for some, it is the first sign of maturity in an otherwise chaotic [psychological and social] experience. . . .

Cordially,

Joel A. Moskowitz, M.D.

Dr. Moskowitz is Acting Clinical Director of Resthaven Psychiatric Hospital and Community Mental Health Center, Los Angeles, California.

Children are running away, across the length and breadth of the United States. For whatever reasons young people are running away, one essential question must be asked—and answered—in relation to them and their predicament: how can they be helped to survive in their plight?

The answer to this question may well rest with the *hotline*. There are two major national hotlines in the United States today. One is based in Houston, Texas; the other in Chicago, Illinois.

THE YOUNGEST OUTLAWS

The first hotline was *Operation Peace of Mind*. It was born in the aftermath of the Houston killings in September, 1973. The phone number is 800-231-6946. (In Texas it is 800-392-3352.)

A year later, the *National Runaway Switchboard* (N.R.S.) opened. The phone number is 800-621-4000. (In Illinois it is 800-972-6004.)

The numbers of both of these hotlines are toll free.

Peace of Mind will also transmit messages it receives by mail. The address is P.O. Box 52896, Houston, Texas 27052. The organization will keep the runaway's forwarding address confidential.

Both lines receive about 1,000 calls a month, about two-thirds from girls. The lines act as a clearinghouse for local hotlines and provide referral information on legal assistance, housing, free clinics, drop-in centers, runaway houses, Traveler's Aid, and the Salvation Army. The hotlines are manned twenty-four hours a day, seven days a week. "Keep trying if the lines are busy," Linda Reppond of the National Runaway Switchboard advises callers.

Another important service the hotlines provide is to act as a neutral link between parents and runaways. Both parents and youngsters can call and leave messages which are kept confidential.

"If a kid calls to ask for a message or help, they don't have to give their name or say where they are," Linda Reppond stated. They may, however, be asked for some information for the purposes of a survey in drawing the national picture of youths on the run. But aid is not dependent on that information, which is kept confidential.

The N.R.S. can also arrange for "conference" calls between parents and runaways. Young people, Ms. Reppond said, may call up and say things like: "I'm in Wyoming. Is there any place I can stay?" Or, "How are things going at home?"

A recent survey on the first six months of the N.R.S. operation shows how the system works. The survey was published by Metro-Help, Inc. It set up and ran the N.R.S. with the aid of federal funds. The survey is based on information supplied by runaways. N.R.S. says it "gathered nearly 3,000 sources of referral throughout the nation, trained a staff and obtained the necessary telephone WATS-lines."

In the first six months, N.R.S. received 6,670 calls. Of these, 3,332 were considered significant. The rest were either calls for information about the services or were prank calls.

Of the 3,332 significant calls, 2,774 were related to runaways. The rest primarily requested other types of youth services (that is, for nonrunaways). "Eight hundred and seventeen calls (24%) came from parents, friends, or relatives of a runaway, and 268 calls (8%) came from agencies working with runaways. The N.R.S. spent an average of twelve minutes with each caller."

In addition, 1,888 youths who called "were actually away from home." Most of these (1,820) were runaways. The rest (68) were throwaways. "This latter figure, representing 3.6% of the total runaway calls," the survey says, "is quite high when one regards the nature of their situation as being abandoned by their parents."

Another 356 calls (14.2%) were from youths who were still

at home, but thinking about running. Two hundred and twenty-eight calls (9.1%) were for runaway information only. The rest, 30 calls (.2%) "were not recorded as falling into any of these specific categories."

Of the 2,244 runaways, pre-runaways, and throwaways, 2,136 (95.1 per cent) "present a clearly defined problem." The survey adds, "Once the N.R.S. worker ascertains the problem, linking the individual up with the proper mode of assistance is a relatively easy process."

According to the survey, problems ("as defined by the caller") included:

Messages	825	36.8%
Housing	476	21.2
Runaway Information	228	10.2
Family Relationships	202	9.0
Legal Aid	102	4.5
Problem Pregnancy	86	3.8
Counseling	59	2.6
Drugs	55	2.4
Long Term Housing	53	2.4
Medical Information	25	1.1
Child Abuse	19	0.8
Suicide	6	0.3
Missing and Undefined	108	4.9

In addition, about 50 per cent of the runaways had crashed with friends; about 31 per cent were on the road; about 10 per cent were with an agency or runaway shelter program; about 5 per cent were with a relative; and another

4 per cent or so were living on their own, the survey reported. The report also stated that the average age for runaways was 16.3, and recidivism was high.

Interestingly enough, the report also notes that many runaways would not tell either where they were or where they were from. Of those who did give locations, 1,335 (nearly 60 per cent) remained in their home state.

In January, 1975, Metro-Help began a follow-up survey of calls received the month before. A total of fifty calls were chosen. These involved the delivery of messages from the runaway to the parents. Workers from the hotline called the families a month after the original message was delivered.

Of the 50 runaways, the survey found, 32 had gone back home within one month. The average length of stay away from home: 18 days. Average distance traveled: 405 miles.

The Switchboard also got favorable ratings from parents and runaways it contacted. Eighty per cent of the parents found it helpful. Ten per cent said it wasn't. Another ten per cent weren't sure if it helped "in establishing a better relationship with their child. . . ."

Of the fifty in the follow-up survey, Metro-Help could only contact twenty-three runaways. But, of those, 91 per cent said the message service was helpful. And "87% said they would use it again if they had to. Only one individual thought our service was not helpful and would not consider using it again," the survey reported.

Metro-Help also identified the type of families involved in its survey. It said that 64% of the families reported they were "intact (having both parents), 34% were 'broken homes' and the remaining 2% did not respond." Most families also identified themselves as being either middle class or working class (42% and 40%, respectively). Another 14% said they were upper class. The rest (4%) either didn't answer or couldn't.

It would seem that the best thing the runaway could do to get help while on the road would be to call a hotline. I continued to pursue the subject of getting help with many of the people I interviewed. "How does a runaway get help?" I asked Brian Slattery of Youth Advocates in San Francisco.

"Everybody's got to answer that for themselves," he told me. "I mean, look around and see . . . the question is: who do you trust?"

What if there isn't a runaway house nearby?

"Okay," said Mr. Slattery, "is there somebody you already know? A schoolteacher, a school counselor, a minister, a local social worker, psychologist, drug program, hot line, drop-in center?"

He also said that he would "check the local mental health association, local suicide prevention, Traveler's Aid. I'd call a community mental health center. I'd call, if I were Jewish, Jewish Social Services. If I were Catholic, Catholic Social Services. Lutheran, Lutheran . . . whoever's got them. . . . Planned Parenthood, if there's one. They're willing to deal with a little more than just sex, or usually know who is."

"A lot depends on what resources are available in your immediate community," Mouse Norris, the former runaway, said. "The first thing to do," he added, "is get off the street. And that is to find some facility: a runaway house, a social worker . . . just call them up on the phone . . . you just say, 'I'm on the street. I don't want to be on the street. But I don't want to go home.' Ask them to look into some places," he advises.

In general, however, it is important to note that the ability of a minor to receive medical help, without parental consent, is limited. This idea is best illustrated by the *Legal Status of Runaway Children* study, conducted by Herbert Beaser and the Educational Systems Corporation, which we quoted from earlier.

"At common law," the author writes, "a minor could not legally consent to be provided with medical or surgical care (except sometimes in certain emergency situations). Although there were exceptions, the consent of the parent or guardian *before* such treatment was required."

Many states do allow for consent by minors who are "emancipated and/or married." They may give "effective consent to medical or surgical care."

Mr. Beaser also notes, however, that "unless a runaway child has been foresighted enough to obtain an emancipation decree before running away from home, such a statute is not likely to be of much assistance to the minor in receiving the needed medical services. Such a statute merely states that an emancipated minor may give a valid consent to medical care. But it leaves the proof of who is an emancipated minor up to the courts in each individual case. And the burden of proof would be on the person asserting the emancipation, in this case, the physician (if, for example, there were a suit for malpractice as a result of the medical care provided)."

However, there has been an easing of the old common law rule that restricted medical help without consent. "In more recent years," Mr. Beaser writes, "many statutes have been enacted giving minors the right to consent to medical care without parental consent for certain situations. . . ."

These situations include "pregnancy, venereal disease, and contraceptive services. The liberalization of some of these statutes relating to the legal ability of a minor to consent to certain medical treatment may prove beneficial. . . ." Mr. Beaser writes. But the legal expert then adds this note of caution. "How beneficial, however, will depend on the availability of the services and the willingness of physicians and surgeons to treat minors who are not known to them and who admit that they are from another state or county."

It is, of course, the job of the hotlines to provide alternatives and referrals for runaways. But the runaway has a job, too. This job is to determine his or her own situation and needs, and to be straight with the people with whom he or she deals.

"Nowadays," Mouse Norris said, "there's a lot of runaway houses and that kind of stuff. And there's a lot of people that are interested in youth problems. . . . But the thing is, you've got to be straight with those people. Like you can't go in there and say your parents burn you with an iron every day *if it's not true*. Because they'll check into it.

"But, then," he also stated, "a lot . . . just depends on the kind of situation you're in. Like if you just ran away to give your parents a shock, it's a completely different situation than running away just because you can't stand it anymore."

The runaway, he said, who just runs to shock his parents will generally end up going home. "But when you run away because you can't stand it anymore, probably the deal is that you're out on the street, and you have no idea what you're doing. You may go home. You may not go home. And it really doesn't matter one way or the other."

Mouse's experience has taught him that "the only way a runaway is going to stay on the street is through sheer perseverance and a lot of luck. A whole, whole lot of luck."

"It's sort of a situation of either they take advantage of you, or you take advantage of them," Joe Wolfenden of the National Youth Alternatives Project (NYAP) said to me when we met in Washington, D.C. (The NYAP published the National Directory of Runaway Centers.) "There really isn't that much of a fair trade that can be developed when you're a runaway . . . it's not very easy for runaways to get in a position of finding employment, where they can really support themselves. If they even really want to do that. . . . A lot of kids say they want to do that, but they don't get around to it," he told me.

"Look," he said a runaway house might tell a youth after a day or two, "you're talking about going to get a job; getting an apartment. But you've been sitting watching the soap operas for three days. And that's not really what you want. You want someone to take care of you. You want to deal with your family. . . . Think about what it is you really want to do."

In this sense then, he notes that "runaways do exploit

people. I mean I was certainly exploited by runaways when they stayed at my house a lot. One of the reasons we started a runaway center was because runaways would rip a lot of people off. . . . So it works both ways. . . ."

"A kid," Marjorie Statman of Runaway House emphasizes, "can stay at Runaway House as long as he is working on his situation."

One consistent theme I found throughout my experiences was the lack of adequate community-based resources for youths. This view was also spelled out by David Palmer of the National Runaway Switchboard. He believes that "there are many areas of the country which do not have these services; where they exist, they are frequently under-budgeted and overworked. Public support of services like these in each community needs to be encouraged."

While there is the belief that there is a trend to community agencies — especially with the decriminalization-deinstitutionalization code of the 1974 federal law we mentioned earlier — traditional agencies cannot be ignored.

But these may again entail the juvenile court. Fr. Bruce Ritter of Covenant House explains: If the runaway is under age and "wants help he can get it. And it's not too hard to get it, if he *wants* it. All he has to do is walk up to a cop and say, 'Hey' . . . most cops will . . . grumble and groan, but they'll take him in. [Or] if he goes to a precinct house. They'll take him in. They have to. And they do. And then the family court immediately gets involved.

"If he's under age and he goes to a police station, they'll take him into custody. And they'll put him in youth house or Spofford House [detention center]. And he'll go to family court the next day. And the judge will try to find a place for him. They'll call Covenant House first. But then the Department of Social Services, if he's under age, will be immediately obliged to investigate the family background to see if he can or should go back home," Father Ritter said.

In some instances then, some observers recommend calling the police. Again, this is an area open to discussion. Says Brian Slattery of Huckleberry House, "I'd *phone* the police [as opposed to going in person without advice and representation of a lawyer] to see what they said on the phone. I would directly ask them what happens. [I'd say] 'Here's my situation. What would happen to me if I came in?' And I think most police would give you the straight goods over the phone."

In some communities, Mr. Slattery adds, there are police who are also trained family counselors. "I can't say a lot; I know of some," he says. But, in "others [communities] you'll get locked up and you have to check it out."

"If a kid is going to run away," advises Onnie Charlton of Runaway House, "the best thing for him or her to do is to run to the runaway house closest to home. Because when we get a kid from Illinois or from any place outside our immediate jurisdiction, there's very little that we can do for that kid. Except direct them back to the runaway house that's nearest to their hometown. In such a case, unless the kid is old enough and responsible enough at that point in his life to go out on his own and get an apartment or job, all of our other services are not applicable. Because we can't do long-term family counseling long-distance, and

173

none of the court services are applicable, because they're from another jurisdiction. And there's no other way for us to pay for the placements that we have, besides the court, unless the parents agree. And we can't even get the parents to agree without a family session.

"So," she says, "the thing we recommend most is for kids to go to the runaway house nearest to home, because that's where the help will get to them.

"The kid," she explains, "in very few places has the right to say: 'There's strange things going on in my family that make me uncomfortable, and I cannot exist here.' Parents have to file an out-of-control petition in order for the kid to get any court help. Or else the kid has to go out and steal a car and be picked up by the police, and the court has to decide to take the kid away from home."

Marjorie Statman agrees. "Even in terms of neglect and abuse cases, it is rough. . . . We've had kids come into this house [Runaway House, Washington, D.C.] where there's been absolutely no doubt in our minds that there's some kind of abuseful or neglectful situation going on at home. And the corporation counsel [for example, the city's lawyer] won't touch it because he doesn't feel like there's enough proof."

This brings us to a major point in the runaway's attempts to get help in resolving his or her situation. While it may be possible for the youth to get help on the road without the parents' permission, this is only a first—although important—step. A runaway cannot (at least in theory) spend the rest of his or her life crashing, panhandling, hitch-hiking. Eventually there has to be some sort of resolution to the problem. The youth will either go home or find alternative placement. And this involves the parents.

There is, Marjorie Statman says, "the reality that kids who are under eighteen [at least in their jurisdiction] have to deal with their parents or whoever they are in the custody of, in order for any alternative to happen. . . . [For example], they need their parents' permission to live in an alternative kind of placement. They need their parents to be in family counseling if that's what they want. They need permission from a social worker, if they're in court custody, to go live in a group home. And so most alternatives that kids come up with, their parents have to be involved in some way. And that's what we counsel towards."

Another agency useful to runaways is Traveler's Aid. "Traveler's Aid," Marvin Engel said, "can help when kids realize they're in over their head." Here, as anywhere else, the quality of the help available varies from place to place.

A runaway might be put up for the night while his or her story is being checked out. Traveler's Aid, Mr. Engel stated, "works with alternative agencies where they exist." These agencies may range from communes to the sheriff's office.

Some Traveler's Aid agencies, Mr. Engel added, have multiple functions. "We're basically a casework agency," he said. Traveler's Aid agencies may be able to help youths either get money to return home or find an alternative living place such as with a relative or in foster care.

Agencies that are part of the Traveler's Aid chain, Mr. Engel explained at his New York office, include family agencies affiliated with the Family Services Association of America.

The situation of notifying parents again comes up. Sometimes the agency may have to call the police, "though we don't see ourselves as stool pigeons." Legally, they are concerned with protecting themselves. If the parents are called, however, then the police don't have to be, Mr. Engel said. But, "strictly speaking—somebody's got to be notified before the kid is housed."

Mr. Engel noted that sometimes police or other agencies will refer runaways to Traveler's Aid as opposed to sending them through the juvenile justice system. On other occasions, he indicated, youths "can use TA as a referral agency and [as] emergency overnight housing legitimately," where it "has arrangements with hotels. Occasionally," too, they may even use an "empty jail cell," where no other facilities may be available in small towns, he said.

Young people find TAs, Mr. Engel added, through the phone book and by word of mouth. They're also found around airports, bus stations, and train depots. When I took a bus, for example, from the San Francisco airport, I recall seeing a phone by the TA desk at the bus station in the city. It was on the wall and, as I recall, it was free.

Traveler's Aid also does active casework, Mr. Engel explained. "In general, what we try to do," is refer the youth, and "actively go with the kid," to a family agency or court.

Traveler's Aid staff will let the parents know, because it's "illegal to harbor" a runaway, but they will "see he doesn't go back home and get beaten up again," Mr. Engel said.

There are, the TA spokesman added, "eighty agencies" that are part of TA, primarily on the East and West coasts. "But we have 800 cooperating representatives" that "will perform services for us." These may include chapters of the American Red Cross and public welfare agencies, he indicated.

It is interesting to note that sometimes young people can aid themselves and others by helping to start a hotline. That's what Dr. Jim Gordon, a psychiatrist affiliated with Runaway House in Washington, D.C., told me. It "might be possible," he said, "for kid and community to get together." The Prince George's County hotline in Maryland, for instance, was created this way.

"A group of professionals and kids looked into hotlines in September, 1971," coordinator Diane Cabot told me. "Our philosophy was, in order for it to be effective you have to have kid input [as a consumer]."

The young people took part, Ms. Cabot says, in publicity activities and helped get grants for the service.

What all this activity may be telling us is that there has come a recognition that running away is often a cry for help that should not be met with silence.

"I think," New York City Family Court Administrative Judge Joseph Williams stated, "we've got to recognize that children have been leaving home as long as we can remember. The new thing is that they are coming into complex situations that are dangerous to them."

Judge Williams asks, "How do we protect them? They're going to move. I don't think that anything we're going to do is to stop a kid from going. He's going to go. Now. How do we protect them?

"Do we have hostels for them? Do we provide [a service] where he can go in and have somebody act as his ombudsman or intermediary? [Who can] contact his family for him and then try to work out his problem? And he doesn't have to swallow his pride in order to get back home. Would [the ombudsman] be his advocate to deal with his parent and follow the dictate of what the youngster would like to have done, so far as these negotiations on his return are concerned?" Judge Williams asks.

The hotlines and runaway centers fulfill some of the above-mentioned needs. But to many people, there aren't enough of these. Observers also feel that the community pays a high price for a lack of concern. "Whether you're interested in how young people are treated, or whether you're interested in the tax base, you should be interested in how status offenders are treated," says John Rector, the staff counsel to Senator Bayh. He adds:

Because if you're not, you're going to end up paying a lot of bucks as a taxpayer every year to house them in institutions when they've never engaged in criminal conduct.

And more likely than not [they] will [engage in criminal conduct] when they come out of those places. The real problem all over the country [is] you go to jail after jail, and find all the young people [confined]. That's bad enough in itself. But then you find them co-mingling with a whole host of characters. It's an education, but it's not exactly what society should be encouraging. [It's an education because these jails act as schools for crime. The young people learn bad habits from the offenders they are mixed with.]

178

On the Road: Getting Help

Mr. Rector acknowledges that community-based facilities (such as ones having a psychiatrist) could be expensive. But SAJA (Special Approaches in Juvenile Assistance) type facilities could be developed that would cost far less than institutionalization in a state training school.

There are no easy answers to the runaway problem. It does little good to attack judges and courts, it is argued, when the society that makes the laws fails to back them up. Such a point was brought home by a long-time family court judge, Justine Wise Polier, now with the Children's Defense Fund. She has written that "the founders could not foresee that the states would establish juvenile courts throughout the country but fail to provide the staffing or placement facilities needed. . . ."

What kind of facilities are needed? Perhaps that was best answered by a former runaway, Mouse Norris. "My idea of a good program," he said, "has to have residence. It has to have [a] street program, with street workers. It has to have crisis counseling. It has to have twenty-four hour phone lines. It has to have good contacts in the social service sector of the government and with the police. You've got to have good contacts with judges. And if you've got that, and good people doing it, people dedicated to what they're doing, you've got a good program, or you've got excellent potential for a good program."

Yet, perhaps, the focus should be more on *preventing* problems before they get out of control rather than on treating them. With the aid of agencies staffed with determined people, conditions could be created where the young people

179

and their families could seek help *before* a youth becomes a runaway.

As David Palmer of the National Runaway Switchboard has written: "The best medicine is preventive medicine, and in that light the best way to deal with a runaway situation is to see that it doesn't happen in the first place."

The road to help has signposts. They are called compassion, communication, and understanding. And this road runs both ways.

10.

Running Away--
Is it the Only Way?

"Get your head together more. Out on the road, man, there are so many perverts. And so many people that are out to just hurt you, you know. And maybe you don't know it, and maybe it's time you found out. But don't find out the hard way. If you don't take to the road, you can get your head together a lot of ways. . . . Like a lot of people don't have the nerve to go up to their parents and say, 'Hey, I'm gonna leave, you know. Because I think you're really a rotten parent.' And they don't give their parents a chance at all to explain why they do things. If your parents really are that rotten, you can talk to a doctor. Maybe if he can't help, he can refer you to someone else who can. . . . Go home. Try to get a job. Try to get your head a little more together. I can't wait until I see my dog again.

"My mother said: 'You think you can live here?' And I said, 'Oh, yeah. I got my head better together than before.'

And she went, 'Well, you know, there are going to be rules.'
And I said, 'Well, that's okay . . . there's rules to everything
you do.' "

Astrid, 17

I met Astrid at Huckleberry House in San Francisco. She
had been jilted by her fiancé and had taken off. Now she
was heading back home and glad to have that chance.

"I called my mother last night," she said. "She asked me
if I wanted to come home. I said, 'Yeah, that's what I'm
calling for.' We get along pretty good. We have things
once in a while, but so does everybody else."

Running away is many times a two-way street. "The
youth is probably just as much the cause as the family is,"
Joe Wolfenden of National Youth Alternatives Project said.
"I mean, the youth probably communicates with the family just as little. Most of it's because of a lack of communication. And the kid probably communicates just as
little as the parents do. . . ." he told me.

Runaways do not exist in a vacuum. They see their roles
within the family as well as their parents' roles in certain
ways.

"I feel it's not really anyone's fault," Leah, a sixteen-year-
old explained. I met Leah at Green House, which is several
blocks from Huckleberry House in San Francisco (and also
connected with Youth Advocates). "The program," house
manager Betty Baskind said, "grew out of a need that was
learned about at Huck's . . . kids who were going to placement or home needed [an] interim place." Counselor
Yvonne Lopez added, "it gives them an opportunity to find

out what they really want and what will meet their needs."

Leah said she hoped to be going home. "We're gonna start family sessions. And hopefully we'll be able to work out our problems. You know, find out what's going on in each other's heads. So that, you know, the problems won't occur again. Well, they will, of course, but then we'll be able to handle them."

"I have a lot of compassion for teenagers," Teaneck Home for Girls housemother Mary Jane told me. "I don't think I had a very good life when I was a teenager. Only I never spoke up to them [parents]. I just let them do what they wanted to. I never ran away. I never talked back. I never said anything. I held it all inside. And now it's all coming out. And I tell them. And they say: That never happened."

How can such tragic misunderstandings between parents and children be avoided? Sometimes it takes direct communication. Other times it takes the intervention of a third party, a neutral person.

David Palmer of the National Runaway Switchboard suggests that "parents need to keep their lines of communication open to find out how their children are feeling about their life, the world around them and their families."

Runaway Denise gives the following advice. "I say talk to your parents. That's the only thing you can do. Try talking things out instead of arguing."

I asked Mouse Norris that if the young person is not sure he or she is going to take off or not, what should the individual do first?

"Wow," said Mouse. "Let's see. Well, before I split, you know, I tried to sit down and talk my father into letting me have some freedom and do some of the things that I was into. And I guess that that would be the best rap."

I wanted to know what might be done if that didn't work.

"Then the next thing would be to probably call the runaway hotline," he advised.

I posed the same question to Brian Slattery of Youth Advocates. "Everybody's got to answer that for himself. I mean, look around and see . . . the question is: whom do you trust? . . . And the question is bigger than that. Who will help me with my family?

"Then I ask," he continued, "well, whom do you and your parents trust? And oftentimes it's clergymen. Or school personnel, who can free themselves from their authoritarian role to be able to hear all sides involved in a dispute. And [who can] give people some kind of feedback and [help in] working it out."

Mr. Slattery also said, "I'd ask other kids who I knew had similar problems. And the reason I say that is . . . most of the kids come [here] because they hear about us from another kid."

National Youth Alternatives Project's Joe Wolfenden adds: "All the traditional family services are there . . . but . . . I think that the commitment isn't there on the part of . . . families—the commitment and the understanding." Mr. Wolfenden told of the father who said: "You want me to talk to my kid now when I haven't talked to him in sixteen years?"

Parent-child communication (or the lack of it) was a very important thing for the young people with whom I spoke. At Teaneck, in particular, the girls mentioned a particular song they liked. It was something they related to. The singer was rock artist Cat Stevens. The song was "Father and Son."

In the song, the son says to the father:

How can I try to explain, 'cause when I do he/turns away again, It's always been the same/same old story. From the moment I could talk/I was ordered to listen, now there's a way and/I know I have to go. . . .
And the father says:
It's not time/to make a change, just sit down take/ it slowly, you're/still young that's/your fault, there's so much you have to go/through. . . .

Pressures affect everyone. Therefore, it sometimes takes a real effort on all sides to work problems out. Or, as Joe Wolfenden says, it takes a commitment.

He stated that "even if the counseling agencies are there, very few individuals, whether they be mother, father, child, sibling are willing to make the kind of commitment [honestly] and to accept . . . what other people's feelings are." Therefore, he adds, "assuming talking to parents doesn't work . . . I think that hotlines serve a pretty valid function as a sounding board. Someone that the kid can talk to. Some only provide referral services. You know, it's hard to go to a counselor for the first time . . . and maybe just talking to somebody anonymously over the phone a few times and then getting some kind of referral to a counselor [might help].

"And," he emphasizes, "the kid should have an understanding that going to a counselor does *not* mean that they are necessarily messed up, but just that there's somebody that they can relate to. A lot of places they can [go to a counselor on their own]. A lot of places they can't. . . . That's why I suggested hotlines. . . ."

One tragic incident of failed communication was told to *New York Times'* reporter James P. Sterba not long ago. This was the story of a runaway girl who called the Operation Peace of Mind hotline. The girl spoke with director Grace Surguy. Sterba picks up the story from there.

"When a runaway girl called Miss Surguy . . . the girl wanted her mother to know she was four months pregnant," Mr. Sterba writes. "Miss Surguy called the mother, who replied, 'I don't want to have anything to do with her.' That message was relayed to the girl when she called back. The crestfallen girl hung up. A little while later, the girl's mother called Miss Surguy, but the girl could not be reached."

It would not be an exaggeration to say that hotlines can serve a lifesaving function. But they cannot cause parents to communicate with children and children with parents if that commitment is not there. In Sterba's story that commitment, for whatever reason—hurt, pain, anger—came too late. But it doesn't have to.

No one says it's easy. Sometimes it's very hard for parents to see that their teenagers need freedom and respect to develop. Sometimes it's very hard for young people to see that their parents have their obligations and responsibilities.

As sixteen-year-old Leah said: "I feel it's not really anyone's fault. It's mine and it's hers. I don't know. Like it's me, I can see it's me, because I do the things that I do. The things that I do that bug her. But then again, she doesn't really help all the time, you know. Like she has her part in it, too. So I'm not saying it's all my fault or all hers, because it isn't."

Before I left, I asked Leah if she had any advice for young people who were thinking of running away. "Well," she said. "I've been on that route before. . . . But you can't run away from your problems. Eventually you're going to get caught. Or you'll come back and you'll have to deal with them."

But Leah left out one important fact: running away is a status offense. Interestingly enough, the only negative reaction to the title of this book was by Len Tropin of the National Council on Crime and Delinquency.

"I would not consider a kid who runs away for a good reason an outlaw. That stigmatizes him. Change the name of the book. Call it 'The Youngest Rebels'," he said.

Perhaps some day Senator Bayh's efforts, as well as Mr. Tropin's and countless others, to have status offenses decriminalized and deinstitutionalized will succeed. Until then, however, runaways will remain "the youngest outlaws."

BIBLIOGRAPHY

Books

Ambrosino, Lillian. *Runaways*. Boston: Beacon Press, 1971.

Bock, Richard, and English, Abigail. *Got Me on the Run: A Study of Runaways*. Boston: Beacon Press, 1973.

Ginott, Haim. *Between Parent & Teenager*. New York: Avon, 1973.

Murphy, Patrick T. *Our Kindly Parent—The State*. New York: Viking Press, Inc., 1974.

Stierlin, Helm. *Separating Parents & Adolescents: A Perspective on Running Away, Schizophrenia & Waywardness*. New York: Quadrangle, 1974.

Wakin, Edward. *Children Without Justice*. New York: National Council of Jewish Women, Inc., 1975.

Wilkerson, Albert E., ed. *The Rights of Children: Emergent Concepts in Law and Society*. Philadelphia: Temple University Press, 1973.

Other Publications

Beaser, Herbert Wilton. *The Legal Status of Runaway Children*. Conducted for the Educational Systems Corp. (Washington, D.C.) for the Office of Youth Development, Office of Human Development, Department of Health, Education, and Welfare, 1975.

Bibliography on Runaway Youth. U.S. Department of Health, Education, and Welfare, Office of Human Development, Office of Youth Development (Washington, D.C.).

U.S. Congress, Senate, Committee on Labor and Public Welfare, Subcommittee on Children and Youth Hearings. 24, 25, 26 September 1973.

U.S. Congress, Senate, Committee on the Judiciary, Subcommittee to Investigate Juvenile Delinquency Hearings. 13, 14 January 1972.

INDEX

ABOUT THE AUTHOR

Arnold Rubin was born in Virginia in 1946, but has lived in New York City most of his life. He has a BA in political science from Hunter College (N.Y.) and an MSJ in journalism from Northwestern University (Illinois).

He has been a Washington correspondent for a couple of radio stations, as well as a newspaper and magazine reporter-editor.

Mr. Rubin has also been a teacher in the New York City public school system and has taught emotionally disturbed children.

In addition, he has been an Emmy Awards' judge (news specials and documentaries), and has traveled the length and breadth of the United States including three side trips overseas.

He has been writing for teenagers since 1971.

With any free time Mr. Rubin can manage, he reads, writes, listens to nearly all kinds of music, plays some chess, walks, and dates.